Pier Paolo Pasolini and the Theatre of the Word

Theatre and Dramatic Studies, No. 60

Oscar C. Brockett, Series Editor

Professor of Drama and Holder of the
Z. T. Scott Family Chair in Drama
The University of Texas at Austin

Other Titles in This Series

Pier Paolo Pasolini and the Theatre of the Word

by
William Van Watson

U·M·I Research Press

Ann Arbor / London

Produced and distributed by
UMI Research Press
an imprint of
University Microfilms Inc.
Ann Arbor, Michigan 48106

Library of Congress Cataloging in Publication Data

Watson, William Van.
  Pier Paolo Pasolini and the theatre of the word / by
William Van Watson.
    p. cm—(Theatre and dramatic studies ; no. 60)
    Bibliography: p.
    Includes index.
    ISBN 0-8357-1975-8 (alk. paper)
    1. Pasolini, Pier Paolo, 1922-1975—Dramatic works. I. Title.
II. Series.
PQ4835.A48Z97   1989
852'.914—dc19   89-4731
                                                                        CIP

British Library CIP data is available.

To Francesca R. and Italo N.

Orgy
The premiere directed by Pier Paolo Pasolini and produced by the Teatro Stabile at the Deposito D'Arte Presente, Turin, November 1968. With Laura Betti as the Woman and Luigi Mezzanotte as the Man.
(Courtesy Associazione "Fondo Pier Paolo Pasolini")

Contents

Foreword

Pasolini once wrote that death performs a lightning-fast editing job on the film of one's life, that it not only gives closure to one's life's story, but that it retrospectively organizes and explains that life, selecting out its salient moments and establishing the hidden logic which governs their progression. Thus, according to Dante's account in *Purgatory* III, Manfred's sin-filled existence, relieved only by a last-minute act of repentance, becomes retroactively a lifelong preparation for conversion rather than the rogue's history it had seemed during the course of its unfolding. Death is thus the privileged vantage point from which life is endowed with meaning, or, as Pasolini was to write in "Osservazioni sul piano seguenza" (*Empirismo eretico*), "Thanks only to death, our life serves to express us."

Such a formulation, however, must be applied with extreme caution to the case of Pasolini, whose death was so untimely and sensational that it could not help but inform any critical assessment of his career. As a murder whose circumstances have yet to be satisfactorily explained, the event invites the kind of interpretation that will necessarily determine a reading of the life that led to so violent a conclusion. Thus, for those who saw the crime as a political assassination, engineered by Pasolini's many enemies on both the right and the left, his life assumes the form of hagiography, of the martyr's biography in which every episode leads inevitably to self-sacrifice in the name of a cause, be it Marxism, sexual freedom, or artistic license. For those who instead saw Pasolini as bent on self-destruction, courting disaster every night when he cruised a city's blighted areas in search of homosexual adventure, his death seemed to come as if by invitation. Some who viewed his death as self-authorized, like Pasolini's long-time friend Giuseppe Zigaina, saw it less as a surrender to an instinctual death-wish than as a conscious decision to give his life a kind of metaphysical coherence.

All such interpretations of Pasolini's end require justifications, and these are to be found in abundance in the biography and the vast artistic production of the man. Thus advocates of the assassination theory emphasize the politically inflammatory aspects of Pasolini's career, while proponents of the "suicide-by-proxy" approach point out the ubiquity of violent death in the oeuvre and the author's occasional prophecies of a tragic personal destiny.

The perspective of the ending inevitably tends to privilege one facet of Pasolini's artistic production over all others—his filmmaking, in which the insistence on physical violence provides the most immediate imagistic analogue to the lurid sensationalism of his own public death. It would be easy to see in the hyperviolence of *Salò*, Pasolini's controversial allegory of fascist power-abuse (and, perhaps not coincidentally, his last film), a limit beyond which not even the filmmaker himself could ever hope to go in the depiction of sexual and homicidal atrocities on the screen.

The acceptance of Pasolini's notion that death works a lightning-fast editing job on life raises two closely related questions. First (to continue the cinematic metaphor), who is to do the editing, and second, how is it to be done without lapsing into reductionism, without subordinating the life to the need for an explanation—in short, without making a thesis film?

William Van Watson's book provides a powerful corrective to such reductionist tendencies in viewing the complex, troubled, and prodigious career of Pasolini. Most significantly, it argues for the vital importance of Pasolini's dramatic production—hitherto virtually ignored by the English-speaking world—to an understanding of the artist's overall cultural contribution. But Watson's book is antireductionist in another, less obvious way. While Pasolini's life and work generate a great deal of critical discomfort because of their contradictions and inconsistencies, Watson never shrinks from these troublesome matters. He accepts the contradictions and sympathetically explores them, refusing to force the writer into a closed critical system. For example, Pasolini lived the contradiction of being a bourgeois who sought to return to a pre-fallen, pre-capitalist state of grace through intimate personal contact with the Roman subproletariat, though this meant exploiting and "consuming" his various partners (one of whom murdered him). He was a narcissist caught in the bind of trying to lose himself sexually in another, though that other was a mirror of the ideal self which he longed to possess.

Not surprisingly, Pasolini's theatre abounds in contradictions. In order to bring about a socialist revolution and abolish class distinctions, the plays address a bourgeois intellectual elite which will in turn "enlighten" the working classes in strict hierarchical fashion. To this end, Pasolini must use reason, the very concept which he so maligns in his poetry and cinema. A more fundamental contradiction involves the deployment of language itself as a vehicle for the conveyance of politically engaged themes, while words are simultaneously found to be nonreferential, self-reflexive, incapable of authentic communication.

A deep ideological contradiction resides at the heart of Pasolini's political thought, which Watson aptly analyzes according to the Oedipus myth. Laius represents the old bourgeois regime, while Oedipus represents the new, revolutionary order that aspires to power. In such an aspiration, of course, Oedipus betrays his desire to become another Laius—yet one more repressive order to be overthrown in its time according to the ancient Rite of Kings. Nor are the revolutionary goals progressive in Pasolini—they involve no linear movement toward a modern, Marxist, industrial state, but rather a return to a Paradise Lost of primitive, agrarian, pre-capitalist ideals. It is this uneasy blend of Marxism and political regressivism which prompts the poet to confess at the tomb of Antonio Gramsci:

> The scandal of contradicting myself, of being
> with you and against you; with you in my heart,
> in the light, against you in my dark viscera;
> ....
> Attracted by a proletarian life
> anterior to you, it is for me a religion
> its happiness, not its millenary
> struggle: its nature, not its conscience.
>
> ("Le ceneri di Gramsci")

Such contradiction, far from blocking Pasolini, seemed to energize him, as did the impulse to pastiche which characterizes the artist's stylistic experiments. Pasolini called his technique "contamination," preferring a term far more charged than the morally neutral concept of pastiche. A contaminated style is one which deviates from norms of artistic purity, and this deliberate invocation of a morally condemnatory term reveals Pasolini's typically provocative stance—a stance which he celebrates in the important essay "Cinema impopolare" (1970). Here Pasolini argues for a filmmaking practice which frustrates the expectations of the two major divisions of the viewing public: those who want conventional spectacle, and those who revel in avant-garde experimentation. But Pasolini refuses to make his films either consumer products or marginalized, "ghettoized" offerings for the intellectual elite, vowing instead to remain on the firing line, to expose himself to martyrdom, to volunteer himself for a *morte spettacolare* (a spectacular death). Such a cinema will appeal only to a select public which can appreciate and participate in the sadomasochistic freedom of the filmmaker liberated from all conventional restraints.

Pasolini's comments in "Cinema impopolare," written two years after his *Manifesto per un nuovo teatro*, are in close accordance with his ideas on the theatre. The liberated playwright, like the liberated filmmaker, must avoid either conventional dramaturgy (the Theatre of Chatter) and the avant-garde (the Theatre of the Gesture or the Howl), opting instead for the more *engagé*, though nonetheless unconventional, Theatre of the Word. It is the very difficulty of these plays that encourages the audience to become an equal partner in the making of meaning.

As Pasolini refused to conform to any conventional categories for cinema or drama, so he fits uneasily into any larger cultural classifications. There is a strong case to be made for the post-modernist affinities of Pasolini's art in its insistence on denaturalizing language, on the openness of the work, and on pastiche. But the deep structure of Pasolini's thought is always the same, and such coherence militates against the fragmented worldview of post-modernism. All Pasolini's plays, as Watson so lucidly demonstrates, tell one basic Ur-story: that of man's fall from a primal state of grace, innocence, mystery, primitive agrarianism, and social justice into a corrupt, bourgeois order of rationalism, stratification, and dehumanizing urban industrialism. As this Ur-story is told in all Pasolini's work, but with particular intensity and clarity in the six plays conceived in one month's time during 1966, it behooves us to study them with the greatest attention if we are fully to determine the organizing principles of Pasolini's art. Watson's book is an illuminating first step in that direction. As such, Pasolini studies in the English-speaking world stand to be greatly enhanced by this rigorous and sympathetic treatment of an unjustly neglected episode in the artist's prodigious career. When Watson writes that "like Pirandello and Ugo Betti before him, Pasolini may first have to establish his reputation as a dramatist outside Italy before he can be canonized as a theatre artist on the Italian stage," he is certainly paving the way for the first critical and scholarly phases of this process. This book makes essential reading for those of us who would become better interpreters, or to use Pasolini's own metaphor, better editors, of the film of his life.

Millicent Marcus

Author's Preface

This work is the fruit of two years' residency in Italy, during which time I had the opportunity to immerse myself in both the Italian culture as a whole and in the Italian theatre in particular, thus providing me with two much-needed contexts in which to place Pasolini's Theatre of the Word. In general, modern Italian theatre is woefully neglected by English-speaking scholars both of the theatre and of Italian studies. Consequently, I have often found myself straddling what are considered two distinct disciplines—Italian and theatre. Furthermore, the study of Pasolini's theatre is rendered more problematic in that it requires a knowledge of both semiotics and structuralism, two schools of critical thought with which most film scholars are familiar, but which remain relatively unknown to many theatre scholars and theatre artists. In any case, Pasolini's plays are certainly interesting and provocative enough to warrant this somewhat synergistic approach.

Pasolini's theatre demands that a variety of critical viewpoints be brought to bear on his texts, most notably Freudian Oedipal psychoanalysis, Gramscian Marxism, Lacanian psychosemiotics and the semiotics/structuralism of Eco and Barthes. In addition, although Pasolini's theatre work is quite distinct from his work in the cinema, comparisons between his filmography and his plays are also often illuminating, and their inclusion makes my critical method more eclectic. This study could have been organized in a more Barthesian manner, subordinating the texts to whatever critical points there were to be made. However, such an approach would have obscured the plays themselves, and as this study must serve as the first English-language introduction to Pasolini's theatre, I thought it imperative that the texts of the plays, rather than the critical perspectives, be the determining factor for the organization of this work. The production histories of the plays are combined in a single chapter, rather than relegated to the chapters on the individual plays, in order to better delineate the evolution of the various practices that Italian theatre artists have employed as they have confronted the task of producing the Theatre of the Word. In fact, in the twenty years since Pasolini's theatre first hit the stage, traditions have been established, such as the fusion of the so-called Ronconian acting method with Italian bravura, the use of musical accompaniment, and a visual design style perhaps best described as "operatic minimalism."

In any case, this book constitutes the most comprehensive study of Pasolini's theatre to date in any language. I hope it serves to encourage production of his texts and to establish his reputation in the English-speaking theatre as a viable and important dramatic artist. His theatrical work is certainly deserving of far more attention than it has received heretofore, as in my estimation, plays such as *Calderón, Affabulation* and *Orgy* rank with the very best the post-modernist world theatre has to offer.

Acknowledgments

I would like to thank Aldo and Elena Roveda, Laura Betti and the Associazione "Fondo Pier Paolo Pasolini," Raffaella Fioretta and the PCI, Italo Nunziata, Carlo Vanni, James Ruscoe, Giuseppe Zigaina, the Oldrini family, the Borgi family, the Ambrosoni family, and Rosella Cercone and the staff of the Biblioteca Teatrale del Burcardo, Rome, Italy.

1

Pasolini and Pasoliniana:
A Psychoanalytic Perspective

Despite their quality, the theatrical writings of Pier Paolo Pasolini are unknown to the English-speaking stage. Outside of Italy, Pasolini's reputation rests primarily upon his work as a film director. Cineastes are familiar with his film theories and many books in a variety of languages have been devoted to his cinema. However, there is perhaps the tendency to relegate him to the art film house, to dismiss him too abruptly as a phenomenon of the 1960s, as the man who championed the use of nudity in nonpornographic cinema, particularly as it was this which, at least in part, gained him international notoriety and a wide audience.

In Italy, Pasolini is known as much for his writings as for his films. He began his career as a poet and novelist decades before he began working in cinema. Although he may not be the most widely read of modern Italian authors in Italy, he is certainly among the most discussed. All Italians know who he was, most have seen his films, and even those who have not read his writings have very strong opinions about him. In fact, Pasolini was probably the most controversial person in post–World War II Italy, eliciting as much condemnation as praise. He noted, "The first duty of a writer is not to fear unpopularity" (qtd. in *Jonas* 16).[1] His incisive and insightful criticism of the modernization processes at work in post–World War II Italy won him enemies among both the authorities and the population as a whole. The majority of his books and films were initially censored and embroiled him in several dozen court cases spanning a period of four decades. Ousted from Italy's communist party (PCI), contemptuous of the political right and accused of everything from pornography to assault, he spurred controversy both in and outside of Italy. His notorious death, the result of a homosexual tryst, became front-page news in literally every Italian newspaper, as well as in the foreign press. Over five thousand people showed up for his memorial services in Rome's Campo de' Fiori, where, ironically, heretics had been burned by the Catholic Church during the Middle Ages.

The attendance at these ceremonies indicates that Pasolini had in fact become a popular figure, despite his relative disregard for popularity. In an era which prized provocation, he found himself Italy's leading provocateur. Despite their initial censorship, his books and films found their audience and won a variety of awards. His reputation as the self-appointed conscience of the nation went virtually unrivalled. Some of his work, such as his films *Teorema* (1968; *Teorema*) and *The Decameron* (1971; *Il Decameron*), even became quite fashionable. Pasolini's death did not lessen the impact he made on Italian society. Pasolini's lifelong friend, the noted painter Giuseppe Zigaina, points out that "it was only after Pasolini's death that the sense of his experience began to emerge from his life and work" (269). This is particularly true of Pasolini's theatre. His ability to endure after his death attests to the sincerity and engagement with which he wrote and worked. Unlike other popular personalities of the 1950s and 1960s, he has not disappeared from the Italian consciousness.

Pasolini's personal friend, the noted novelist Alberto Moravia, explains, "Success . . . came or did not come, but he didn't do anything purposely to achieve it; his goal remained, as always, the desire to express himself" ("Sade"). Despite Pasolini's incessant interest in the social and political issues of his day, it was probably his desire to express himself which proved to be the more pervasive motivation for his writing. In a letter Pasolini confesses, "As for my sins . . . I think of nothing else so much as my work" (qtd. in *Oggi*, 13 November 1985: 42). In the poem "Poet of the Ashes" (1967; "Poeta delle Ceneri") he claims to have done nothing but write ferociously from the time of his arrival in Rome in 1950 until his ulcer attack in March 1966. Pasolini was not only a compulsive writer but also a prolific one. His body of work includes six books of poetry, six novels, eight plays, two translations of plays, sixteen films, screenplays for other directors such as Federico Fellini, Mauro Bolognini and Bernardo Bertolucci, and a vast array of books and articles of literary, artistic, social and political criticism.

In any creative process there is some sort of relationship between the art work and the life of the artist who creates it. This relationship is particularly noticeable in Pasolini's early works. In fact, one of his post-humously published early novellas, *My Love* (1982; *Amado mio*), is actually a diary. His poetry of the 1940s and 1950s often reads like a series of intimate confessions recounted with powerful immediacy. Such works stem directly from Pasolini's compulsive, therapeutic need to write. This relationship between Pasolini's life and art becomes more obtuse in his later works, wherein his attention turns to the agendas of a variety of critical approaches, such as Gramscian Marxism, Freudian psychoanalysis, Italian neo-realism, structuralism, semiotics and experimentalist linguistic hermeticism. As a result, his work of the 1960s and 1970s is often more enigmatic and removed from the specifics of his own life than the work of his youth. Nevertheless, Zigaina maintains, "Pasolini always and invariably wrote about himself" (270). Autobiographical references do, in fact, persist in his later works and can be found in all his plays. The play *Beast of Style* (1979; *Bestia da Stile*), for instance, functions as an intellectualized autobiography of his aesthetic development as a writer.

In any case, as Pasolini's life did influence his art, it merits some discussion. Pasolini was born on 5 March 1922, in Bologna, the first of two sons to Carlo and Susanna Pasolini. His father was a professional military man whose career demanded that the family move frequently from one town to another, thus preventing the young Pier Paolo from making friends, and contributing to the sense of isolation he was to feel throughout his life. The best source of information on his childhood is an interview he granted his personal friend, the noted feminist writer Dacia Maraini, for *Vogue* magazine. In the interview he describes a classical Oedipal tension between himself and his father. He recalls a traumatic confrontation: "When my mother was about to give birth, my eyes began to hurt and burn. My father held me immobile on the kitchen table, opening my eye with his finger and giving me the eyedrops. From that 'symbolic' moment on I stopped loving my father" (131). The description presents an image of the father who phallically violates his son with the eyedropper. Interpreting the scene in Freudian terms is not amiss, as Pasolini himself saw the encounter as "symbolic." The Roman psychologist Aldo Carotenuto argues, "In many of the writings a knowledge of Freud appears, and it is legitimate to suppose that Pasolini had read the works on psychoanalysis" (21). Indeed, Pasolini makes a ready use of Freud in much of his work and his own life falls into the Freudian Oedipal model with great facility, as he himself realized.

It is interesting that in the above account Pasolini associates the burning of his eyes with his mother's pregnancy. He remembers having asked her how children are born, hearing her frank and honest answer and refusing to believe her. His refusal to believe her constitutes a classic homosexual rejection of the mother as animal. Instead, she is an ideal being, seen to exist only in the symbiotic mother-infant relationship as an extension of the infant himself, a projection of his secondary narcissism. Pasolini describes his view of his mother during his early years as "a half-memory, invisible," that is, as lacking an identity distinct from his own (qtd. in *Vogue* 131).

Pasolini's younger brother, Guido, was born when Pier Paolo was three years old, the age at which the Oedipal phase theoretically begins. The following year Pasolini began sleeping in the same bed with his mother. His identification with her became disproportionate, as he himself would later confess. In 1942 he wrote, "While thinking about her I am overcome by a painful fit of love; she loves me too much and I love her too much" (qtd. in Carotenuto 18). By the very sweetness and sincerity of her nature she was, as Carotenuto puts it, "omnipotent and omnipresent" with Pasolini (104). His idealization of his mother is evident in the many poems he wrote to her and in his casting of her as the Virgin Mary in his film *The Gospel according to Matthew* (1964; *Il Vangelo secondo Matteo*). In 1950 he ran away with her to Rome as if they were a pair of lovers, leaving his father behind in the Friuli region. Pasolini thus played Oedipus to his father's Laius, replacing his father in the affections of his mother. Accordingly, in his play *Affabulation* (1977; *Affabulazione*) he would later observe, "Fathers, you know, are all impotent" (103).

Pasolini's disproportionate Oedipal love for his mother corresponded to the feelings of Oedipal animosity he had for his father. A military man, a fascist and a man of the sword, Carlo Pasolini was the perfect authority figure against which Pier Paolo could rebel, becoming in his own turn a deserter, a communist and a man of the pen. The drunken, aggressive scenes the elder Pasolini made only served to strengthen the bond between mother and child. The feminist Adele Cambria describes "the rapport of solidarity that sprang up between the mother (oppressed) and the son (oppressed) within the patriarchal family structure." Identifying with the young and oppressed Oedipus, the infant abandoned in the woods, the man who would be king, Pasolini was to challenge authority and champion those whom he considered oppressed for most of his life.

Susanna read to Pier Paolo when he was young and inspired in him a love of literature. He began writing at the age of seven. When he was fourteen he read what he called his first "adult" book, *Macbeth*, the story of another Oedipus figure who deposes an older king. After moving about northern Italy in his childhood, as a teenager he settled with his family in the small town of Casarsa in the agrarian western part of the Friuli-Venezia-Giulia, Italy's northeasternmost region, which borders on Austria and Yugoslavia. The town was home to his mother's relatives.

In 1942 he published his first book, *Poetry for Casarsa (Poesie a Casarsa)*, choosing to write in the Friulan dialect that he associated with his mother, considered by many Italians to be the most beautiful of Italian dialects. (Actually, Susanna Pasolini's immediate family spoke a dialect of the neighboring Veneto region.) The dialect offered Pasolini not only a beautiful language, but also the opportunity to spite his father who could not understand it. His use of dialect also defied fascist authority, as the government of the time discouraged the use of dialects in an effort to mold a more unified national Italian identity. In effect, Friulan functioned for Pasolini as a sort of Oedipal language, a natural language indigenous to the populace, as opposed to the more formalized, structured and official Laius language of Italian.[2] Pasolini wrote a second book of poetry, *The Better Youth* (1954; *La meglio gioventù*), and his first play, *The Turks in Friuli* (1980; *I Turcs tal Friùl*), in the Friulan dialect as well. These works, along with his posthumously published early novels *My Love* and *Impure Acts* (1982; *Atti impuri*), and the later novel *The Dream of a Thing* (1962; *Il sogno di una cosa*), evoke a Friuli fully within the pastoral tradition, a land of innocence, a latter-day Eden. These works create what Moravia calls Pasolini's "peasant myth." In contrast, the Friulan landscape and temperament are actually among the most austere in Italy. In a very Romantic way, Pasolini had projected his own emotions onto the landscape and people of the region. He later realized this in his poem "Returning to the Country" (1975; "Tornant al pais") wherein he writes, "You deceived me, the life was in me, you were a shadow, and a shadow was your fire" (*Gioventù* 180).

Pasolini recalls first being attracted to boys during the period immediately following his brother's birth, but it was not until the war years in the Friuli that his homosexuality first came to the fore. While his father fought with the fascists and his brother fought with the partisans, he and his mother opened a school in the Friuli. His first love, whom he dubs "Nisiuti" in his diary-novel *Amado mio*, was one of his students. His attraction to his male students would later embroil him in a scandal which cost him his position in the PCI and resulted in his self-imposed exile from the Friuli.

While Pasolini idealized his love for the blond Nisiuti, his first truly sexual experience was with a dark soldier from southern Italy whom he calls "Bruno." Throughout his career he would continue to identify dark Latin types with animal love and fairer, blond types with spiritual love. Accordingly, the dark Franco Citti plays the womanizing lowlife in the films *Accattone* (1961; *Accattone*) and *Mamma Roma* (1962; *Mamma Roma*), while the blonder, blue-eyed Terence Stamp is the mysterious, spiritual visitor in *Teorema*. This tendency can also be seen in his plays, as the Father in *Affabulation* is obsessed with the unearthly blondness of his son's hair and the Woman in *Orgy* (1979; *Orgia*) wants to be sexually violated specifically by a southern immigrant. These stereotypes are common in Italian culture as a whole, as southerners are often considered to be more virile, but tall Aryan types dominate the men's fashion industry in Milan as the idealization of male beauty.

The writings of Pasolini's youth are infused with an intense Romanticism. He tells Nisiuti, "Your beauty is so infinite that neither the human voice nor discourse, not even the looking at you . . . manages in any way to express what you are" (*Amado* 97). Pasolini's love for Nisiuti was never consummated and remained spiritual in nature. However, eventually Pasolini could no longer sustain this idealized love. He writes in despair that ultimately "no other love mattered to me than that of the flesh" (*Amado* 82). Pasolini's love for Bruno was such a love, animalistic in nature, but the soldier deprived Pasolini of the opportunity of developing any emotional attachment. Theirs remained little more than an encounter. Love, as the fusion of animal and spiritual, was the Romantic means by which Pasolini sought to reintegrate what he felt to be his divided self. However, he remained divided between Bruno and Nisiuti, as neither alone provided him with a love that was both animal and spiritual, as neither alone provided him with a sense of Romantic transcendence.

Ultimately, both Bruno and Nisiuti were merely projections of Pasolini's own secondary narcissism, the same secondary narcissism which had caused his inordinate attachment to his mother. There are numerous references to Narcissus in his poetry of the Friulan period, and some of the poems even have the Greek character's name in their titles. He writes about Nisiuti, "There were days in which I was completely in him, in which I was nothing else but his smile, one of his expressions. Only my eyes remained for contemplating him" (*Amado* 98). Pasolini seeks to lose himself, or to find his other self, in Nisiuti, but the process remains incomplete even as his love went unconsummated. His eyes remain. Narcissism is itself symptomatic of man's divided nature, as Narcissus is at once the object he observes and the observer himself. Part of the self remains outside the self, not fully integrated. It is precisely this sensibility which permeates much of Pasolini's writing and his plays in particular.

The French psychoanalyst Jacques Lacan's concept of the "mirror stage" illuminates this sense of alienation inherent in narcissism, particularly as it manifests itself in the work of Pasolini. According to Lacan, the mirror stage is concurrent with the fall from the sense of wholeness experienced in the symbiotic mother-infant relationship. At this time, the infant becomes physiologically capable of focusing on objects outside himself, most notably his own image in a mirror. He perceives in this image a unified wholeness which he cannot experience subjectively; instead, he has only a fragmentary awareness of his own body (i.e., mouth, fingers, feet, etc.), as he attempts to exercise motor control. Lacan calls this fragmentary sensibility *corps morcelé*, the body in pieces. Stylistically, this theory explains Pasolini's interest in the pastiche form. It also addresses the obsessive dismembering of bodies in his filmography, and his concern with fetishism in *Teorema* and *Medea* (1970; *Medea*) in particular.

The discrepancy between the perceived wholeness of the other and the fragmentary nature of the self provokes the psychological phenomenon of transitivism, the identification of the self with the other, Lacan's interpretation of Rimbaud's "I is an other" (23). Whereas Pirandello interprets this "I is an other" sensibility in almost existential terms, Pasolini sees in it the primordial, spiritual fall of man. Virtually all the protagonists of his plays are plagued by this sense of "I is an other," and it certainly characterizes the intensity of his feelings for Bruno and Nisiuti. Consequently, although Pasolini's love for Bruno and Nisiuti may have constituted a transgression, Pasolini defends himself with a quotation from the Italian Romantic writer Ugo Foscolo to close his diary-novel. Foscolo writes, "Guilt is purified by the heat of passion" (qtd. in *Amado* 125). The intensity of Pasolini's desire for the other, in this case Bruno and Nisiuti, corresponds to his own sense of lack of being, his awareness of his incomplete, divided and fragmentary self.

Throughout the diary-novel Pasolini ascribes a cosmic significance to his love for Bruno and Nisiuti as a means of rationalizing, validating and defending it. Because of the keen sense of transgression and guilt that informs much of Pasolini's work, it has often been interpreted from a distinctly Catholic perspective by critics, many of whom have not investigated the matter in its roots. Pasolini himself claims to have ceased believing in God at the age of fourteen. Even prior to this he had not been especially religious. Neither of his parents were avid churchgoers and, according to his own account, his family was too bourgeois to be tinged with any sort of fanaticism. However, during the war years, inspired by the fear of bombings and the fear of his homosexuality being discovered, Pasolini came to believe in God, in a God of wrath, a Laius figure with omnipotent cosmic authority. He describes "an inexorable presence of God ... neither goodness nor justice, but pure fatality" (*Amado* 26).

At the same time he observed the blind faith and the Catholic cultural rituals of the Friulan peasants which he later described in *The Dream of a Thing*. Through contact with the Friulans he came to believe in a "first Father who had the sweetness of a Mother" ("Ceneri" 21). This God was antecedent to the God of wrath. He was not a Laius figure but a nurturing entity with whom Pasolini could identify as he had identified with his own mother. The androgyny of this "first Father" corresponded to the early symbiotic mother-infant relationship which Pasolini had valued so disproportionately. In a Lacanian sense, assigning God a gender paradoxically reduces Him into an imperfect entity, as the existence of separate sexes indicates their individual incompleteness. As this "first Father" was the original God, preceding the fall, he could not have individual gender. In this manner Pasolini rebelled against the authority figure of a male God just as he rebelled against the Laius figure of his own father.

Pasolini wrote, "Religion, religion as a direct rapport with God still exists in the world anterior to that of the bourgeoisie" ("Ceneri" 21). The world of the Friulan peasant was one such "anterior world." However, even after his Friulan period Pasolini remained fascinated by the naive and primitive religions of pre-capitalistic societies. His films *Oedipus the King* (1967; *Edipo Re*), *Medea* (1970; *Medea*), *The Gospel according to Matthew* and *The Decameron* all reflect this fascination. However, being bourgeois, he could never really fully accept these religions for himself, and his interest in them was ultimately more cultural or anthropological than spiritual, as the four above-mentioned films also demonstrate.

However, the source of the guilt which Pasolini needed purified by the heat of passion was not really religious, nor even existential; instead, the source of his guilt was social, rooted in the behavioral codes of the bourgeoisie which he knew did not condone his homosexuality. Pasolini responded by accusing the bourgeoisie of having lost any real sense of reverence for the sacred, of having discarded the mystery of religion in favor of its own behavioral codes, codes which could ostensibly be empirically or rationally verified. In contrast, in accord with Romantic tradition, Pasolini asserted the importance of passion. He saw that the fear of the unknown no longer inspired man with the awe of pre-capitalistic religions. Instead, modern man responds to this fear with a cowardly retreat into conformity and the use of reason. Like Lord Byron, Pasolini viewed the world as winding down from an ancient and prehistoric grandeur, as it approaches a gray stasis. For Pasolini, this devolution was essentially a social process which, nevertheless, had spiritual effects and implications. The result is what the critic Enrico Groppali calls a "Univocal Undifferentiated Chaos" (*L'ossessione* 86).[3]

Like George Bernard Shaw, Pasolini blamed the deterioration of religion, and by extension the universe, on Pauline Christianity. Pasolini comments, "St. Paul has been the great disgrace of this little world" ("Dansa di Narcìs," *Gioventù* 219). St. Paul's epistles include codes of behavior, rules and reprimands to those who failed to observe these rules, rather than a discussion of religion as a spiritually transcendent or primordially ecstatic rite. The legacy of St. Paul is basically a lay religion wherein institutionalism flourishes by replacing reverence with obedience; as such, it has been embraced by the bourgeoisie. In the novel version of *Teorema*, Pasolini writes that "the bourgeoisie . . . has substituted the conscience for the soul" (177). Pasolini did not consider this a viable substitution, as the conscience was a product of man's divided self, consciousness of the self being prerequisite to it. As such, the conscience is a reminder of man's fall and his exile from Eden rather than a vehicle for transcending this fall.

Carotenuto observes, "Pasolini always seemed to be moved by the same intimate need: to enter into a rapport with the most immediate, primitive and original . . . aspects . . . of the world in which he lived" (15). Having rejected the degenerate, fallen God of the bourgeoisie, and incapable of fully immersing himself in primitive religions, Pasolini sought the "immediate, primitive and original" in sex. He writes, "I believe in God the Father, the Son and the Holy Spirit, I believe in tender lips and strong hands. I believe in the Church and in the fourteen-year-old boys who smilingly masturbate on the banks of the Tagliamento River: there where St. Paul never reached in his voyages" ("Pastorela di Narcìs," *Gioventù* 220). In the passage Pasolini fuses sexual and spiritual images, even as he attempts to integrate the spiritual self by achieving an integration of the animal self, by manipulating the libido. Orgasm becomes a means of subverting the consciousness, self-consciousness and conscience that are symptomatic of the divided self, a division which both St. Paul and bourgeois society exploit. Pasolini used sexual union as a vehicle for religious unity in *Teorema*. A similar sense of visceral religiosity marks the opening sacrifice in *Medea*, Giotto's dream at the end of *The Decameron*, and the whole of *The Gospel according to Matthew*, as well as the plays *Orgy* and *Affabulation*. In this context, masturbation represents an attempt to unify the self with the self, a sort of libidinal narcissism. Masturbation, like homosexuality, is a non-procreative form of sexual behavior, as neither results in offspring which would serve as a living reminder of man's individual mortality. The need for offspring merely reflects man's imperfect nature and fall from grace. In contrast, Pasolini has "a vision of unfruitful and . . . pure love" ("La realtà," *Le poesie* 355). The love's purity is proved by its very unfruitfulness.

Pasolini's interest in the "immediate, primitive and original" in pre-capitalistic societies eventually became not only religious, but social and political as well. He found in the theories of Marx and Engels the same Romantic nostalgia for the peasant world that he had infused in his Friulan writings. Marx and Engels wrote about a world in the process of being uprooted by industrialization, a world in which man was being "disintegrated" by the forces of social change around him. Pasolini witnessed these same changes in post–World War II Italy and so joined the PCI, despite the fact that his brother had been killed by Yugoslavian communists. He took an active role in the workings of the local party in the Friuli until the scandal of his sexuality led to his expulsion from it in 1948. Nevertheless, Pasolini's communism was to flourish more fully in Rome, where he at first lived in abject poverty on the outskirts of the city.

Under fascism many Italians had been legally bound to remain in their hometowns, but after the war thousands migrated to Rome in hopes of a better life, only to find themselves in shantytowns outside the city. During the two decades after World War II, Italy went through the same social, demographic and industrial evolution which had taken Great Britain two centuries to complete. More than being a period of progress, it was a period of upheaval on a massive scale. Living in the shantytowns of Rome, Pasolini encountered the grim world of the sub-proletariat, a substratum of society composed primarily of the unemployed, those who worked only occasional or odd jobs, and those involved in petty crime. Living in shacks with dirt floors, no heating and no public utilities, the subproletariat was a social nightmare the Italian authorities would have liked to have forgotten.

It was this substratum of society which inspired the neo-realism of Fellini's *The Nights of Cabiria* (1957; *Le notti di Cabiria*), Vittorio De Sica's *Shoeshine* (1946; *Sciuscià*), and the Neapolitan episode of Roberto Rossellini's *Paisan* (1946; *Paisà*). Cesare Zavattini, the leading theorist of the neo-realist movement, advocated a renewed engagement of the arts with the harsh social realities of the time. Such an approach was in stark contrast to the empty escapism which had blighted the Italian cultural scene during fascism. Italy's leftist intellectuals came to the fore as Marxism became fashionable. Novelists such as Elio Vittorini, Cesare Pavese and Italo Calvino all gravitated toward the political left and even joined the PCI for a period of time. Vittorini's *Men and nonmen* (1945; *Uomini e no*), Pavese's *The Comrade* (1947; *Il compagno*) and Calvino's *The Path to the Nest of Spiders* (1947; *Il sentiero dei nidi di ragno*) all praise the common man and celebrate the partisan struggle against the fascist order. In cinema, a variety of directors, including Luchino Visconti and

Michelangelo Antonioni, thrived as they espoused communist philosophies. Pasolini kept the phenomenon in perspective. He wrote, "The problematic individual who presented himself as a 'committed' artist was given full citizenship rights in Italy for a period of time. His acceptance was merely the alibi behind which the bourgeoisie hid its own guilty conscience" (*Empirismo* 130). In fact, film directors eventually discarded the impoverished characters of neo-realism, preferring instead to address themselves to the guilty conscience of the bourgeoisie in a more direct manner. The problems of basic survival in such neo-realistic films as Visconti's *The Earth Trembles* (1948; *La terra trema*) and Rossellini's *Germany, Year Zero* (1947; *Germania, anno zero*) were replaced with the more existential concerns of the affluent characters of such films as Fellini's *La Dolce Vita* (1959) and Antonioni's *Red Desert* (1964; *Il deserto rosso*). In literature, the overt social engagement of neo-realism was devalued in favor of a retreat into literary hermeticism. Such hermeticism can be distinguished in the *Gruppo '63*'s neo-experimentalist interest with formalistic concerns, and also in the self-conscious semiological sense of play in Calvino's later writings and Leonardo Sciascia's detective novels.

Pasolini himself was relatively late in coming to neo-realism and relatively late in leaving it. He wrote his two novels *The Ragazzi* (1955; *Ragazzi di vita*) and *A Violent Life* (1959; *Una vita violenta*) in the neo-realist style, as well as his film scripts for Fellini and Bolognini. His first two films, *Accattone* and *Mamma Roma*, were also done in this style. He discarded the Friulan peasants for the "immediate, primitive and original" that was to be found in the inhabitants of the shantytowns. He replaced the Friulan dialect with *romanaccio*, a sort of city-speak which evolved among the immigrants in Rome as their own dialects were mutually unintelligible. Far from the effusive latter-day Romanticism of his Friulan works, Pasolini's writings of this early period in Rome are characterized by a cold, almost disturbingly detached objectivity.

Despite his seeming objectivity, Pasolini asserted, "I consider my neo-realism an act of love" (qtd. in Carotenuto 13). Here love is neither animal nor spiritual, but political and social, as Pasolini sought engagement with the world around him rather than within himself. Pasolini became the champion of the politically unaware subproletariat, playing the classic role of the communist intellectual who fights for the rights of an oppressed and ignorant populace. Pasolini established a rapport of solidarity with this oppressed class as he had with his mother. He identified with the subproletariat on the sexual level as well, preferring liaisons with boys from this class until his death. Ettore Garofolo, Franco Citti and Ninetto Davoli, actors whom Pasolini used repeatedly in his films, all came from this substratum of society. Pasolini maintained lifelong relationships with them and other members of the subproletariat, assigning to them, as to himself, the role of the oppressed Oedipus.

Unlike many writers who have concerned themselves with the problems of the poor, Pasolini did have extensive firsthand experience with them, but ultimately he was not one of them. He was a bourgeois who had attended the prestigious Università di Bologna, the oldest university in Europe. Most of Rome's subproletariat came from the south, but Pasolini had grown up in the Veneto and Emilia-Romagna regions of the north. To the extent that Pasolini was bourgeois, he was not an Oedipus, but a Laius figure, a man with power, as he himself realized: "I would belong, in the end, to that ruling class" ("La realtà: poesie mondane," *Le poesie* 339).

However, this was a role he could not accept. He wrote, "I couldn't convince myself that there was anything to love in a bourgeois" ("O me donzel," *Gioventù* 171). He could not reconcile his real-life Laius background with his Oedipal self-image. The self was again divided, and Pasolini led a double life alternating between his nocturnal escapades and his role as a respectable bourgeois intellectual. As a result, many critics have discerned self-hate and self-destructiveness in his work. By the 1960s he was middle-aged and had already achieved fame, fortune and the status and power of a true modern-day Laius figure. Nevertheless, he insisted, "Nothing is changed: I still see myself as poor and young: and I love only those who are like me" ("O me donzel," *Gioventù* 171). As the Laius role asserted itself over his identity, he responded by pursuing young boys from the subproletariat in an increasingly desperate attempt to mirror himself narcissistically in the Oedipal role.

In the early 1960s Pasolini abandoned the social consciousness of neo-realism for the more universal realities of myth. He translated Aeschylus' *Oresteia* for the acclaimed Italian actor Vittorio Gassman and directed the film versions of *Oedipus the King, Medea* and *The Gospel according to Matthew*. These films offered Pasolini the opportunity to investigate societies "anterior to that of the bourgeoisie," as well as allowing him to explore the Jungian primordial and communal subconscious, an area of irrational truth which the objectivity of the neo-realist aesthetic had excluded from him. To a certain extent neo-realism had inhibited Pasolini; it was an aesthetic he had adopted rather than developed for himself. Its objectivity relied on the uninspired use of reason that he associated with the bourgeoisie. For inspiration and an understanding of irrational truth Pasolini turned to myth. He defended his interest in myth as being neither escapist nor nostalgic, claiming that "only that which is real is mythic, and visa-versa" ("Comunicato all'Ansa," *Le poesie* 617). The film *Teorema* functions as a sort of modern-day myth, and the plays *Pylades* (1977; *Pilade*) and *Affabulation* both take specific Greek myths as their points of departure. In fact, a mythic sensibility permeates Pasolini's work from the mid-1960s on.

However, the most notable change in his work of the period is that, like Visconti and Fellini before him, his attention shifts directly to the bourgeoisie. This is particularly true of the plays. The critic Gian Carlo Ferretti explains what may have motivated Pasolini to discard his sub-proletariat characters for bourgeois protagonists:

> Parting from the conviction . . . that his world (and myth) of the subproletariat as a fundamental part of the anti-bourgeois revolution was disappearing, he began to believe that no real collective opposition, no real uprising *within* a capitalist society was possible any longer. ("L'autopunizione," in Luzi 293)

Pasolini had been an early proponent of the Italian Marxist writer Antonio Gramsci's theory of hegemony, that social classes can eventually gain political power by first exercising their influence through cultural and civil institutions. However, as postwar Italy prospered, Pasolini came to realize that the lower classes were not winning such hegemony within Italian society.

Nineteen sixty-eight proved to be a pivotal year, as Pasolini despaired that the student rebellions of the period were not only ineffectual, but also insincere. He unexpectedly took the part of the police employed to suppress the rebellions, pointing out that the police were the sons of the proletariat, while the students were bourgeois, rebelling because it was fashionable to do so, although they may have believed themselves to be firm in their convictions at the time. Pasolini termed the rebellions an "intestinal struggle," a means by which the bourgeoisie exorcises its communal guilt. Most of his critics have since conceded the accuracy of his insight into the situation. The critic Giuliano Manacorda comments, "In other words, bourgeois society expressed these oppositions to itself, then reintegrating them into its own category" ("Speranza," in Roncaglia 81). Indeed, youthful rebellion proved and has continued to prove itself to be highly marketable, providing inadvertent support to the bourgeois establishment it purports to attack, even furthering the growth of this establishment. The Oedipal threat has been neutralized by the Laius power figures of the modern bourgeoisie. The potential Oedipus figures, the youth, are actually performing the Laius role, although perhaps unknowingly so.

Ferretti continues with the observation:

> The bourgeoisie—by now victorious and empty more than ever before of idealistic value—had no other function left but that of becoming fully self-conscious and recognizing its own guilt, and therefore the necessity of its own self-condemnation and self-destruction. (293–94)

The self-destructiveness of the bourgeoisie can be seen in a variety of Italian films of the late 1960s and early 1970s, such as Bertolucci's *The Conformist* (1970; *Il conformista*), Visconti's *Death in Venice* (1971; *Morte a Venezia*), De Sica's *The Garden of the Finzi-Continis* (1970; *Il giardino di Finzi-Continis*) and Liliana Cavani's *The Night Porter* (1974; *Il portiere di notte*). Virtually all the bourgeois protagonists of these films condemn and destroy themselves in some way, as they attempt to internalize the Laius-Oedipus polemic. The same holds true for Pasolini's own bourgeois-oriented films of the period, namely *Teorema* (1968) and *Pigsty* (1969; *Porcile*). As his plays were conceived from this same sensibility, each of them contains an apocalyptic vision of the bourgeoisie as a whole destroying itself, and taking the rest of the world with it into oblivion. For Pasolini, this apocalypse results from the fact that the bourgeoisie serves only to further man's fall and the division of the self, suppressing or neutralizing both man's animal and spiritual natures by taking refuge in the intellectual and the rational.

In his so-called "trilogy of life" films, *The Decameron, The Canterbury Tales* (1972; *I racconti di Canterbury*) and *A Thousand and One Nights* (1974; *Il fiore delle Mille e una Notte*), and, to a lesser extent, in the play *Calderón* (1973; *Calderón*), he investigates the origins of the bourgeoisie and its interface with the peasant and aristocratic worlds which preceded it. The trilogy challenged the censorship codes of the time with its scenes of full frontal nudity and its frank celebration of the sexual drive as an integral part of the human spirit. Although at least the first two films of the trilogy contain a decidedly communist polemic, this was too often ignored as the trilogy was heralded as a simple emblem of the sexual revolution. Pasolini found that his own rebellion had become integrated into the bourgeoisie, as a number of soft porn exploitation films purporting to emulate Pasolini's formula sought the commercial popularity that the trilogy had attained. The profit motive replaced artistic expression.

When the bourgeoisie had managed to reduce Pasolini's "trilogy of life" to serve its own ends, he responded with one of the most controversial films in the history of cinema, *Salò, or the 120 Days of Sodom* (1975; *Salò, o le 120 giornate di Sodoma*). The bourgeoisie has still not managed fully to reintegrate the film and possibly never will, as showing the film remains a matter of contention in many places. The film was attacked for viewing everything in specifically sexual terms, something which Freud had already done two generations earlier. Pasolini responded, "Sex is nothing other than a political problem" (qtd. in *Il Messaggero* 2 November 1976). Pasolini views human behavior from a sociobiological perspective distinctly his own. Whether dealing with sex or with politics, ultimately Pasolini is addressing the issue of power. He asserts that "that which characterizes power—any power—is its natural capacity to transform bodies into things" (qtd. in *Jonas* 24). He certainly demonstrates this in *Salò*.

Salò can be read as a metaphor for modern bourgeois society. Be it fascist or capitalist, this society is based upon a power structure which is arbitrary and no longer rooted either in the natural values of strength and beauty or in values associated with some sort of larger cosmic order. Instead, the bourgeoisie flourishes because it has discarded the Great Chain of Being and the concept of the divine right of kings. It establishes itself on the assumption that man is in a fallen state, severed from both himself and God, and that there is no natural order inherently within the universe. The bourgeoisie profits from this perceived void by constructing its own power system to fill it, a power system which is both hermetic and precarious in nature. Pasolini paraphrases the Marquis de Sade, claiming that "nothing is more profoundly anarchic than power: and that applies for every power" (qtd. in *Jonas* 24). Power is anarchic because it presupposes a disintegration of the universe, a lack of wholeness and unity, in order to establish a hierarchy of its own. The society of *Salò* is a pointedly artificial construct, stratified, a hierarchy wherein there is a very rigid semblance of order, an order which Pasolini exposes as being nothing other than organized anarchy.

Capitalism bases its order and hierarchical structure upon the principle of money. Capitalism is antithetical to humanism inasmuch as it pits man against man in a competitive environment, while communism theoretically bases itself on sharing and mutual cooperation in an effort to create a classless society. Historically, it is capitalism which has given rise to the modern ruling class of the bourgeoisie. In capitalism money is power. In his later life Pasolini had this power and, ironically, it also led him to transform bodies into things, as he bought sexual favors from boys.[4]

One such encounter resulted in Pasolini's death. On the night of 2 November 1975, Pasolini picked up the teenaged Pino Pelosi, a boy from the subproletariat, outside the Termini train station in Rome. According to Pelosi's own account, they agreed to an encounter involving oral sex for the sum of twenty thousand lire (approximately $30–$35 at that time). However, Pelosi claims that when they arrived at a soccer field in the beach town of Ostia, Pasolini had other ideas:

> He wanted to play the male. I refused and ran away. . . . Pasolini jumped on top of me. "You ugly pig," he said. "What! You're calling me a pig?" Since he was on top of me, I cut loose with a kick to his face in order to free myself and I got up. Then Pasolini took a stick and hit me in the head. (qtd. in *Il Messaggero* 4 November 1975)

The truth of the story is a matter for conjecture, but in any case the squalid details are unsettling. What is known for sure is that Pasolini was struck a blow to the head and was then run over with his own car, which Pelosi was later seen driving. Pelosi commented almost in disbelief, "I who am nothing killed such an important man" (qtd. in "L'assassino"). The remark reflects the peculiarly Oedipal nature of the murder, in which Pasolini finally could not avoid playing the Laius role.[5]

In the first chapter of his biography of Pasolini, Enzo Siciliano makes a strong argument that Pasolini's death was a political assassination for which Pelosi served as bait. This theory tends to turn Pasolini into a martyr, and various groups, most notably the communists and homosexuals and, to a lesser extent, the feminists, have attempted to claim him as their own. However, Pasolini can hardly be regarded as a martyr for the communists. His relationship with the party had been problematic since the days of his sexual scandal in the Friuli. His political vision transcended party loyalties and he had been scheduled to speak at a meeting of the Italian Radical Party when he died. His film *Anger* (1963; *La rabbia*) opens with a virulent attack on the Soviet Union's invasion of Hungary in 1956, and the novel *The Dream of a Thing* satirizes the naive communist idealism of its young heroes. Nevertheless, both the PCI and the Federation of Italian Communist Youth (FGCI) have honored Pasolini as a communist, and some communists are intent on reinstating Pasolini within the party system itself.

Pasolini cannot be regarded as a martyr for homosexuality either, as he never really championed it as a cause during his lifetime. Although homosexuality is a recurrent theme in his early poetry and in his plays, it rarely comes to the fore in his filmography. While *Teorema* might seem to present homosexuality in something of a positive light, *Salò* and the "trilogy of life" films openly attack it. In fact, Pasolini never fully integrated his homosexuality into his personality. It served only to augment his already keen sense of self-alienation. He comments, "My homosexuality was something additional, something outside, it had nothing to do with me. I always viewed it beside me as my enemy" (qtd. in Carotenuto 25). Nevertheless, Pasolini is fast becoming part of the gay chic in Europe, gaining himself the same audience which has helped catapult Genet to popularity. Articles have appeared on Pasolini in gay magazines, and his face served as the cover for an issue of the Italian gay periodical *Babilonia*.

Admittedly, Pasolini was a homosexual and he had been a communist party member, but he was never a feminist, as Cambria and others have attempted to argue. Although the play *Calderón* might seem to support Cambria's assertion, Pasolini was no simple liberal. He opposed abortion and disapproved of the greater freedom Italian girls were gaining in choosing their role in life. Maraini, who knew him for many years, claims he thought of young girls primarily as rivals for the young boys he pursued. For him, feminism merely contributed to the disintegration of the natural order. In fact, a strain of misogyny can even be discerned in his work, from *Accattone* to *Orgy*. It was not womanhood but motherhood which Pasolini idealized. Pasolini's strong, positive female characters are all mothers rather than feminists. Rosaura in *Calderón*, like Mamma Roma and Medea in the films of the same names, all fall into the mold of this maternal ideal.

In the final analysis, Moravia's assessment of Pasolini's death is probably the most accurate. He observes, "Pier Paolo died as one can die falling in front of a tram: in an accident like any other. Every day there are thousands of homosexual encounters in Italy: Pier Paolo died in one of these" (qtd. in Siciliano, *Alberto* 97). Too much attention has been diverted from the significance of Pasolini's work to the significance and sensationalism of his death, probably because of an obsession with death which pervades much of his writing. Carotenuto has even asserted, "Death is the real protagonist" in Pasolini's works (20). It is a decidedly recurrent theme in his poetry, and many of his films and plays conclude with the deaths of their central characters.

However, despite this obsessiveness with death, Pasolini should not be discounted as a simple pessimist or reactionary. What Pasolini could not resolve in the content of his work, he nevertheless continued to attempt to resolve in the form of his work. Even in a work as despair-ridden as *Salò* there is a celebration of form, of the artistic process itself. Carotenuto claims that for Pasolini the "creative act was lived as a divine act" (82). Pasolini certainly presents inspiration as being divine in nature when Giotto has his vision at the conclusion of *The Decameron*. In any case, when confronted with a world with "all coherence gone," as John Donne put it, Pasolini, unlike the existentialists of his generation, did not simply accept this absence of coherence as a given. Instead, he persistently attempted to retrieve coherence in his art, either by means of a late Romantic concern for transcendence and unity, or else by a post-modernist sense of hermetic structuralism. In fact, this search for coherence, for God, for transcendence, not only informs his art, but also, for him, virtually becomes the artistic process itself.

2

The Contemporary Italian Theatre: An Historical Perspective

If Pasolini's theatrical writings are unknown to the English-speaking stage, contemporary Italian drama as a whole has fared little better, particularly in the United States. Dario Fo has managed to enjoy some individual triumphs in this country, most notably during his 1986 tour, but he has not found here the large following he has cultivated throughout much of Europe. Eduardo De Filippo is popular in Great Britain, but he has not been widely produced in this country. In the 1950s Ugo Betti was a major influence on the French existentialist dramatists, and the English critic Henry Reed considered his dramatic talent superior to Pirandello's, but productions of his plays in the United States are sporadic at best. Dino Buzzati's *A Clinical Case* (1953; *Un caso clinico*) is comparable in both style and quality to the work of Friedrich Dürrenmatt and the better French Absurdists, but the play remains in obscurity in the English-speaking theatre. In the United States, Gabriele D'Annunzio's reputation as a poet has grown to overshadow his work as a dramatist, although he dedicated much of his career to the theatre. With Eleanora Duse, arguably the best actress of her time, he had a number of successes early in this century, but his plays are practically forgotten in American theatre circles. If Luigi Chiarelli is remembered at all, it is only as Pirandello's predecessor, and the list of Italian playwrights who are relatively unknown to the English-speaking stage continues. Although the works of these playwrights often are not masterpieces, they are of such quality that, had they been part of the French or German theatre, they would have found a place on the English-speaking stage. To an unjustly large extent, twentieth-century Italian theatre means Pirandello and little else to American audiences. Texts in English on the twentieth-century Italian theatre virtually do not exist. One of the few such books is Lander McClintock's *The Age of Pirandello*, which discusses a number of dramatists of Italy's fascist era, all of whom have since been justifiably forgotten by the Italians as well as the rest of the world. McClintock also ineptly censures the best dramatist of the period, Betti, for being too intellectual.

To a certain degree the relatively poor reputation of contemporary Italian theatre may be deserved, but certainly not to the extent to which it has been taken. Italians themselves often speak disparagingly of their theatre. Maraini refers to an "Italian inferiority complex" in this context (*Fare* 42). Texts on contemporary Italian theatre are somewhat scarce in Italian as well. Silvio D'Amico, founder of Italy's Accademia Nazionale d'Arte Drammatica and the country's most prominent theatre critic in the first half of this century, devotes a significant amount of attention to the contemporary Italian theatre in his four-volume history, but since his death in the 1950s information on the subject has been less well organized. Perhaps the best text on the contemporary Italian theatre is Dacia Maraini's *To Make Theatre: Materials, Texts, Interviews* (1974; *Fare teatro: Materiali, testi, interviste*), in which she displays a clarity of thought and expression which is quite rare in Italian theatre criticism.

The greatest problem of the contemporary Italian theatre is its lack of respect for dramatic literature. Of the seven theatre schools operating in Italy during the 1985–1986 academic year, none of them offered courses in playwriting, and only the school of the Piccolo Teatro of Milan offered instruction in dramaturgy. The 1985–1986 theatre season also reflected this lack of respect. Instead of Feydeau, a play called *Cafe Feydeau* was produced; instead of Shakespeare, there was a play called *Shakespeare and Me*; instead of Molière, there was *Molierissimo*. Finally, two groups decided to produce plays about Pasolini's life, *Another Day in '56* and *From the Tagliamento to the Aniene*, rather than Pasolini's own theatrical texts. Interestingly, although such productions saw fit to ignore the work of these dramatists, they also demonstrate a fascination with the playwrights themselves, with the cult of the persona, the cult of genius. Indeed, Italian theatre in general is preoccupied with the cult of genius, often failing to appreciate its own dramatists of merit who may not be geniuses but are nevertheless competent and talented. A minor work by Goldoni or Pirandello usually receives far more attention than a major work by Chiarelli, Betti or Diego Fabbri. Although many Italians may consider Pasolini a genius, it is more for his polemical writings than for his theatre, which too often is ignored. However, Italians frequently are not the best judges of their dramatic writers. Betti first created a sensation in Paris before he came into vogue in Italy, and Pirandello was hardly a driving force on the Italian cultural scene when he received the Nobel Prize for Literature, as his greatest successes had come when he toured his company outside of Italy.

Moravia has argued, "There does not exist, nor has there ever existed a theatre outside of literature, written by people who were not men of letters" (qtd. in Auglas 5). Moravia seems to assume that literary talent and dramatic talent are one and the same thing. This idea may seem absurd to English-speaking theatre artists who know of the dismal dramatic efforts of such noteworthy writers as D. H. Lawrence and Henry James. However, much of the Italian theatre of merit is literary in nature, be it poetic, such as the theatre of Tasso, Alfieri and Manzoni; or philosophic, such as the theatre of Fabbri, Betti and Pirandello; or both, such as the theatre of D'Annunzio and Pasolini. The literary origins of Italian theatre date back to the Renaissance academies. From Machiavelli to Pirandello, the latter of whom is known in Italy as much for his novels as for his plays, the body of Italian dramatic literature has been dominated by men of letters with few exceptions. Pasolini's decision to turn from writing novels and poetry to writing for the theatre is thus not unusual.

The literary nature of Italian dramatic literature is due, at least in part, to the artificiality of the Italian language itself. Based upon the Tuscan of Dante, Boccaccio and Petrarch, the language did not become the official language of Italy until the unification of the country in 1870. Even then, dialects predominated, as only 22% of the country was literate and only 5% of the population understood the formal Italian language (De Mauro, *Storia*). France, Spain and Austria had divided up the Italian peninsula for centuries and this lack of cultural and linguistic unification confounded the Risorgimento sentiment of such writers as Alfieri, Manzoni and Silvio Pellico as they attempted to write for the theatre. The *commedia dell'arte* circumvented this problem by relying on gesture, lazzi and readily recognizable character types. Goldoni avoided the problem by writing in the Venetian dialect. In this century, De Filippo relied on Neapolitan, prompting Maraini to observe, "The only living theatre is dialect theatre" (qtd. in "Gli scrittori" 9).

However, the contemporary situation is actually quite different. Moravia asserts:

> The spoken and literary languages have come closer together. In the novel, the symbiosis has existed for some time. I am convinced that it won't be long in coming to the theatre as well. . . . Language is not a prejudicial obstacle to a national dramatic repertory. (qtd. in Auglas 4)

In fact, although the majority of the Italian populace was still illiterate at the end of World War II, by the 1980s Italy's literacy rate was higher than the United States'. The massive internal migrations which occurred during the economic boom of the 1950s homogenized the population and dialects began to disappear. By the mid-1950s only 20% of the population spoke dialect exclusively, and the trend has since continued to the point where many young Italians do not even know dialect (De Mauro, *Linguaggio* 9). The advent of television has served to accelerate this process.

Opposing attitudes taken toward Realism also account for the comparative neglect the Italian theatre has received in American theatre circles. Virtually all the important twentieth-century American playwrights have gravitated toward Realism. At Elia Kazan's urging, Tennessee Williams suppressed an early interest in Strindberg to write more fully within the Realist vein. Eugene O'Neill eventually discarded his experimentation with Expressionism and Freudian psychology to write in the Realist mode. Realism has been the standard from which dramatists such as Arthur Miller and William Saroyan all-too-consciously deviate. In Italy, on the other hand, Realism came and went in a generation. The late-nineteenth-century Roberto Bracco was heralded as "the Italian Ibsen," but he has been completely and perhaps justly forgotten in this century. The only Italian Realist play to be produced with any degree of frequency in Italy is Giuseppe Giacosa's *Like Falling Leaves* (1900; *Come le foglie*).

This same disregard for Realism also holds true for Italian acting. While American acting has been dominated by methods derived from Stanislavsky and Lee Strasberg's Actors' Studio, Stanislavskian-based technique was considered little more than a vogue by many Italian theatre artists. The former head of Italy's Accademia Nazionale d'Arte Drammatica, Raul Radice, comments, "A public school such as ours cannot be a school of any particular tendencies, such as those of Copeau or Stanislavsky, which were conceived for private institutions" (qtd. in Di Giammarco 30). Instead, Italian acting reflects the cult of genius. Di Giammarco describes Gassman's approach at his Bottega Teatrale theatre school in Florence, "He still sustains, and who knows whether or not it is as a provocation, that talent is the fundamental element, innate and unjust and that schools perhaps serve only to give something to those who already have it. He is not entirely wrong; in fact, he is right" (5). Italian theatre stresses talent over technique, thus maintaining active contact with nineteenth-century traditions. D'Amico describes these traditions in his article "From Actor-Manager to Director" ("Dal capocomico al regista"):

> The *mattatore* company was constructed around the personality of a great actor (sometimes two, one male and one female) who chose the plays to be performed as

a pretext for presenting his own personality. Let it be clear that this did not necessarily always mean a programmed lack of respect for the author, especially if he was a poet; very often the great actor was in good faith, believing himself to be in service to that poet, to understand him as no one else before him had understood him, interpreted him or expressed him. However, apart from the foreseeable blunders coming from an inadequate education or the fatal arrogance of his temperament or irresponsible vanity—he naively believed that in order to interpret the drama only one character was needed. . . . The *mattatore* reduced the drama to a monologue: all the other performers, be they mediocre or bad or worse, had no other function than that of "giving him his cues." (qtd. in Pacuvio 15)

Mattatori are still very much part of the Italian theatre scene. Vittorio Gassman and Gigi Proietti are generally considered to be *mattatori*, as they both direct and play the protagonist in their productions, casting the minor roles from their respective theatre schools. Paolo Poli and Dario Fo also fall within this tradition, not only directing and acting, but also writing their own texts which are specifically designed to showcase their particular talents.

Most English and American critics probably would not take (and, in fact, have not taken) a favorable view of this persistence of traditions which are considered outmoded in the English-speaking theatre, but Italian audiences demand a level of bravura in acting which most English-speaking audiences would reject as pure egoism. They expect "larger than life" performances because they are keenly aware of the role-playing in everyday social reality. Pasolini observes, "The archetype of the theatre occurs before our eyes every day in the street, at home, in public meeting places, etc. In this sense social reality is itself a performance that is not entirely unaware of its being such and has, therefore, its own code" (*Manifesto*, in *Centauro* 143). When Italians interact, they employ a highly developed set of codes, rich in facial expression and gesture. The film director Orson Welles has commented that all Italians are actors (Barzini 62). Italian drama has exploited this awareness of role-playing in society, as Chiarelli and Pirandello have based their theatrical output on viewing life as a performance.

Because of this "larger than life" sensibility, much of Italian theatre has been appropriated by Italian opera. Italy's best theatrical directors— Luchino Visconti, Luca Ronconi, Franco Zeffirelli and Mauro Bolognini, to name a few—either have dedicated or are dedicating a sizable portion of their careers to the opera. Opera receives greater governmental subsidization in Italy than does the theatre. Far from being considered an elitist art form, opera is embraced by most Italians as a part of their national heritage. Not only their temperament, but also their rhythmic language, with its words ending in vowels and its stress on the penultimate syllable, lends itself readily to opera.

In turn, Italian opera has worked its influence on the Italian theatre. The Italian word for acting is *recitazione*, meaning "recitation," and Italian acting is often critiqued in much the same manner as the singing of an operatic *recitativo*. Like the singer, the actor is judged primarily on his ability to perform, rather than on his ability to represent. Accordingly, most Italian theatre productions are underscored with music. Paolo Terni, professor of music history at the Accademia Nazionale d'Arte Drammatica, refers to "an intense reflection of the musical dimension in acting" (qtd. in Di Giammarco 33). Indeed, most Italian actors play with rather than against the musicality of their language, exploiting it as another means of heightening their performance, as no Realist aesthetic inhibits them from doing so.

The artificiality of this emphasis on musicality is rooted in the artificiality of the Italian language itself, as for centuries Italian actors were forced to adopt formal Italian instead of using the dialects which were natural to them. Pasolini comments, "The actor obeys theatrical conventions, not linguistic ones" (*Manifesto* 143). Formal, musical Italian is one such theatrical convention. However, Pasolini defends the practice, attacking the pursuit of Realist verisimilitude as an unrealistic aesthetic delusion. He claims that critics "do not realize that when they say 'spoken language' in referring to an author they are referring to nothing else but a stylized mode of speech in every case" (qtd. in Auglas 6). Shaw and Chekhov may both be Realists, but ultimately Shaw's characters speak Shavian and Chekhov's characters speak Chekhovian. No matter how lifelike art may aspire to be, it is still art and still demands a suspension of disbelief. Italians are very aware of this, even as they are aware that life can be artlike.

Although the *mattatori* persist and profit from such an aesthetic sensibility, the cult of the genius in the contemporary Italian theatre probably revolves more around the directors than the actors. Maraini notes, "Our theatre lives for the presence of a few prestigious directors who stupefy us with their dazzling scenic inventions every time they mount a play" (*Fare* 45). The art of modern directing in Italy dates back to the work of Max Reinhardt and Jacques Copeau, both of whom directed a number of productions in the peninsula during the 1930s. Their work helped pave the way for the establishment of the Accademia Nazionale d'Arte Drammatica, which was founded as a school of directing in 1935. The result is that Italian theatre has evolved into a director's theatre. Unfortunately, this evolution has served only to perpetuate the Italian lack of appreciation for Italian dramatic literature. The theatre artist Roberto Mazzucco explains the situation in an interview with Maraini:

> The director has had a very important function in the de-provincialization of our theatre since after the war. But he has ended up by taking everything in hand, making slaves of the actors and eliminating the author. By now he is the only one who makes a decision in the theatre and this cannot help but damage the theatre itself. . . . Directors have become so powerful and authoritarian that in reality they don't want to know anything about the playwrights. For them playwrights represent rivals. (qtd. in *Fare* 48)

The fact that Pasolini was one of only two Italian directors to direct one of his plays during his lifetime should be viewed within the context of Mazzucco's observation. The Italian theatre scene does not encourage playwriting, as directors often write their own scripts in order to avoid having to work with their playwright "rivals." Their plays, which Siciliano dubs "confections," serve them primarily as a pretext for displaying their own directorial bravura. Few of these works ever merit or receive a second production.

Italian directors tend to neglect dramatic texts of literary quality because they are more concerned with the art of visualization. Pasolini asserts that Italian directors "limit themselves to giving a decorative and formalistic interpretation of the text" (qtd. in Auglas 7). This emphasis on the visual is inherent within the Italian culture itself, as the history of Italian painting, sculpture and architecture is much richer than its literary heritage; in contrast, the quality of English literature generally overwhelms that of English painting. The Italian emphasis on the visual has long had its place in the Italian theatre, not only with the *commedia dell'arte* and the various puppet theatres of Venice, Naples and Sicily, but also within the formal theatre. From Sabbattini to Giacomo Torelli to such dynasties as the Bibiena family, Italian theatrical design dominated western theatre for centuries. In this century, Italian interest in the scenic element has led them to use their Greek amphitheatres, Roman arenas, and Renaissance and Baroque theatres on a regular basis, depending in part on their suitability to the play to be produced. This sensitivity to theatre space extends to their use of open-air locations, such as gardens and piazzas, a practice popularized by Reinhardt.

The Italian eclecticism in theatre space corresponds to their eclecticism in the choice of plays they produce. As Italian directors avoid their Italian playwright "rivals," they frequently turn to foreign dramatists whose work they can conveniently adapt to their own directorial purposes, not contenting themselves with a simple translation. For the same reason, many Italian theatre directors also gravitate to dramatists of the past. The 1985–1986 Italian theatre season, for example, was dominated by Shakespeare, Goldoni, Pirandello and contemporary British playwrights. Moravia assesses the result of the Italian theatre's failure to promote contemporary Italian drama; he writes, "The public in Italy thinks that what is going on on stage has nothing to do with them in any way" (qtd. in "Gli scrittori" 10). Unlike Italian neo-realist film, the post–World War II Italian theatre has not been actively engaged with the political and social realities of the country.

Many of the avant-garde Italian theatre movements of the 1960s ostensibly aimed at reengaging the Italian theatre with the problems of Italian society. However, the theatre continued to be perceived as art and artifice, and therefore remained removed from these social realities. As early as the 1950s, Moravia had already dubbed the Italian avant-garde theatre "the theatre of avant-yesterday" (qtd. in Pandolfi 215). Nevertheless, in the 1960s experimentation did flourish, responding to the influence of Brecht, Grotowski and the Living Theatre. Unfortunately, this experimentation was itself a form of escapism, failing to create a truly engaged theatre. Maraini comments, "The eyes of the groups are turned outside the country. . . . There is little or nothing that is Italian. Even the themes of political theatre deal more with foreign issues (the Vietnam War, Nazism, the commune, the French Revolution, etc.) rather than with Italian ones" (*Fare* 41).

Attempts were made at political theatre, but they were generally considered to be futile. Giuliano Vasilicò, one of the leading avant-garde theatre artists of the time, notes:

> Not that these groups want to turn themselves to the bourgeoisie, but their buyer is the bourgeoisie. Because the bourgeoisie is better educated and has the free time and free money the proletariat lacks. . . . Unfortunately, the proletariat culture of today is television culture. Who can manage to pull the proletariat away from the television? (qtd. in *Fare* 290)

By the 1960s the Italian proletariat had been absorbed into the same capitalist social structure which had given rise to the bourgeoisie. Laborers had evolved into lower class consumers, and a political theatre such as that theorized by Erwin Piscator and Bertolt Brecht two generations earlier no longer seemed possible. Various groups, such as Dario Fo's troupe, performed in meeting halls and for unions, but ultimately avant-garde political theatre was simply just another manifestation of the "intestinal struggle" of the bourgeoisie. Pasolini writes that "the theatre of today is of two types: bourgeois theatre and anti-bourgeois bourgeois theatre" (*Manifesto* 140).

Confirming Pasolini's observation, the more traditional bourgeois theatre responded to the popular and commercial successes of such artists as Fo and Vasilicò by attempting to appropriate their social and political engagement, but only after reducing it to a directorial style or method. Giorgio Strehler, head and cofounder of the Piccolo Teatro, can be credited with popularizing Brecht in Italy, but he did so while remaining firmly within the Italian tradition of a director's theatre, preoccupied with visualization and the artifice of theatre itself. Maraini comments, "The productions that our commercial theatre offers us are vulgar but with refinement, light but with seriousness, superficial but with pedantry, reactionary but with revolutionary flirtations" ("Il momento" 15).

Like the commercial theatre, the avant-garde Italian theatre perpetuated the lack of respect for dramatic literature within Italian culture. The avant-garde of the 1960s in the world as a whole produced few dramatic texts of lasting value, and the Italian avant-garde was no exception. Theatre became almost wholly visual, paving the way for such Italian art performance groups as Falso Movimento and Krypton, which were to thrive in the 1980s. Siciliano writes, "Plays have been destroyed or reduced to pantomime" (qtd. in *Sipario* May 1973: 63). The verbal element was virtually eliminated from many avant-garde theatre productions of the l960s, such as Memè Perlini's highly touted *Pirandello, Who's He?* (1973; *Pirandello, chi è?*). Pasolini describes a performance of the play, "The word is closed inside a box, wrapped and adorned" (qtd. in *Fare* 69).

Moravia, Maraini and Siciliano, all Pasolini's personal friends, sought to salvage the word. In 1966 they created a theatre company housed in the Teatro del Porcospino in Rome. Their expressed purpose was to foster Italian playwriting and a politically and socially engaged Italian theatre. Because of his sensitivity to dramatic texts, Roberto Guicciardini was chosen as director. Unfortunately, the Italian government withdrew subsidization from smaller theatre groups in 1968. The company at the Porcospino thus went bankrupt and was forced to close after only two seasons during which they had received mixed reviews. Although Pasolini never took part in the venture, many of the group's aesthetic and theatrical concerns were also his own.

Moravia divided twentieth-century theatre into two traditions, what he termed the "symbolic" and the "dialectic" traditions. In the first, the drama exists primarily within the subtext rather than the text. Dramatists who wrote such works would include Chekhov, Maeterlinck, Beckett, Pinter and Albee. Such an approach eventually results in the elimination of the text itself as superfluous, as in the theatre of

Robert Wilson. Writers of dialectic theatre would include Shaw and Brecht. In dialectic theatre the drama is externalized into words, which are not used as signifiers of something else, but are themselves the signified, the most direct manifestation possible of the dramatic action. Moravia explains, "I place myself in the second category without hesitation: I am for the text, for the drama put into words; I am not in favor of symbolism, that is, I am not in favor of characters speaking banalities and at the same time investing these banalities with enormous importance" (qtd. in Serenellini 70). Ionesco parodied such banal dialogue in his play *The Bald Soprano*. The Swiss dramatist Dürrenmatt disdained it; he commented, "Many people have lost appreciation for rhetoric since . . . some actor who was not sure of his lines discovered Naturalism. That loss is sad" (qtd. in Clark 315).

Indeed, Realism and Naturalism have contributed to this "lost appreciation for rhetoric," as they have emphasized the subtext and internalization. Perhaps because Realism and Naturalism have never really flourished in Italy, a dialectical theatre has managed to persist there. Both Chiarelli and Pirandello created a dialectical theatre by contrasting their characters' social role-playing with their more natural inclinations. A generation later, Betti and Fabbri continued this dialectical tradition of philosophical argumentation, as both dramatists came to the theatre from legal careers and created the so-called Theatre of Moral Trials. Moravia states, "I took up the direction of Pirandello and other such writers, and I have purposely written plays in which there are ideological and even philosophical arguments and questions" (qtd. in Serenellini 70).

However, the existence of dialectical theatre in Italy has been somewhat sporadic, and it has hardly dominated the contemporary Italian theatre scene as a whole. Pasolini lamented its failure to do so:

> The theatre has lost the word. It has become deaf and dumb. Of an angelic and paralyzing deafness. Of a violent and devastating dumbness. . . . The theatre of today expresses itself in images that are continually more sublime, abstract and diabolic, as well as more suggestive and less meaningful. (qtd. in *Fare* 66)

Pasolini held the avant-garde and the more traditional bourgeois theatre equally responsible for the disappearance of the word from the Italian stage. In his *Manifesto for a New Theatre* (1968; *Manifesto per un nuovo teatro*) he called the avant-garde theatre the Theatre of Gesture or Howl, and the more traditionally commercial theatre he dubbed the Theatre of Chatter. He claims that the Theatre of Gesture or Howl sacrifices the word to "scenic action." He views Artaud, the Living Theatre and Grotowski as having promoted such a theatre. On the other hand, the Theatre of Chatter uses the banalities criticized by Moravia, Ionesco and Dürrenmatt. It incorporates perhaps too many words into its productions, rendering them superfluous to the dramatic action.

In addition to criticizing the Theatre of Gesture or Howl and the Theatre of Chatter for neglecting to appreciate the word, he also faulted them for failing to be truly engaged theatres. He calls the Theatre of Chatter a "theatre of evasion . . . a SOCIAL RITE" (*Manifesto* 143).[1] Such a theatre primarily serves a social function; the bourgeois attends it because doing so is in accord with his social role. On the other hand, Pasolini considered the avant-garde theatre to be self-absorbed, a "theatrical rite" which was ultimately engaged only with the art of the theatre itself. Ironically, such a theatrical sensibility eventually dissects the theatre and evolves into something else. Artaud becomes therapy and the Living Theatre transforms itself into a political demonstration, while a theatre such as that promoted by Grotowski "ends up by becoming an authentic form of modern religion" (*Manifesto* 141). To remedy the situation, Pasolini advocated a theatre which was engaged and availed itself of both the beauty and the communicative potential of the word.

3

The Manifesto for a New Theatre and the Theatre of the Word: A Theoretical Perspective

Pasolini attended neither the Centro Sperimentale Cinematografico nor the Accademia Nazionale d'Arte Drammatica. In fact, he disdained academism as limiting, and created instead both a cinema and a theatre which were as unconventional as they were distinctive, unhampered by preconceptions as to the nature of either art form. Consequently, many Italian critics have been perturbed by both. The critic Gualtiero De Santi stipulates, "Pasolini undeniably proposes neither more nor less than the overthrow of the practices and ideas upon which the theatre has been built for centuries. The provocativeness of the *Manifesto* could not be more absolute" (89). Indeed, much of the criticism levelled at Pasolini's theatre has concerned itself with whether or not it is theatre at all. The critic Rinaldo Rinaldi asserts, "This theatre forswears the 'minimal conditions' for the existence of theatre" (300). Of course, the "minimal conditions" required for the existence of theatre depend largely upon the theatrical conventions of the time. Coming to the theatre from outside the theatre, Pasolini was able to circumvent these conventions.

Pasolini himself had doubts as to the theatrical viability of his plays. He notes, "I consider the theatre, in the manner in which I make it, merely as a particular form of literature. . . . And therefore I also am wrong" (qtd. in Auglas 7). Pasolini's theatre has consequently often been viewed as closet drama, as an extension of his poetry. In fact, Pasolini was motivated to turn to the theatre because of a renewed interest in writing poetry. He comments, "For a long time I haven't written verse and now I love to write theatre in verse. I manage to write verse again provided that I can express myself through the characters and not in the first person. This is the reason I write theatre" (qtd. in Auglas 7). Indeed, the lyricism of his Friulan period had virtually disappeared from his more polemical poetry of the mid-1960s. He rediscovered this lyricism in his verse drama. Nevertheless, he did intend for his theatre to be produced. He observes that "its production . . . would constitute an almost impossible undertaking, but this does not mean it should not be attempted" (*Centauro* 129). Pasolini himself produced and directed *Orgy* in Turin in 1968, and he was planning on producing *Pylades* at the Teatro Fenice in Venice when he died.

Pasolini's interest in the theatre in 1966 may, at first glance, seem sudden, and his relationship with the theatre was problematic. He admitted, "I go to the theatre very little, and every time I swear I won't go back again" (qtd. in "Gli scrittori" 11). Nevertheless, he did go back several times. In 1966 he was no novice to the theatre, having written *The Turks in Friuli* back in 1944, which he later directed for the Teatro Stabile del Friuli. Many of the characteristics of Pasolini's later plays can be found in this early work. The play is covertly autobiographical, there is a dialectic involving both God and politics, dialogue is highly poetic, and violent action occurs offstage and is narrated onstage. A few years later he wrote *Internal Story* (*Storia interiore*), which was not to be produced until 1965 under the title *In '46!* (*Nel '46!*).[1] This was followed by his translation of Aeschylus' *Oresteia* for Gassman in 1960, and finally by a translation of Plautus' *The Braggart* (*Il vantone*) in 1963.

However, all this theatrical activity was at best sporadic, and it was not until he suffered an ulcer attack in March 1966 that he turned his attention fully to the theatre. For a month after the attack he was confined to a hospital bed. It was during this period of convalescence that he began to write the plays, which he then continued working on intermittently until 1974, when he finished the last one, *Beast of Style*. However, Pasolini was too involved with too many other projects to commit himself fully to the theatre for long. In fact, even while still convalescing in the hospital, he had already begun the novel version of *Teorema*. The plays and *Manifesto* of the 1960s were to remain his last theatrical output.

Pasolini's *Manifesto for a New Theatre* first appeared in the periodical *Nuovi Argomenti* in January 1968.[2] The date is important inasmuch as Pasolini had conceived of the plays prior to this time. Consequently, the plays were not written in order to illustrate or support the theories Pasolini proposes in the *Manifesto,* something which some critics have asserted. The critic Pia Friedrich claims that the *Manifesto* "has made its mark on the history of the Italian theatre" (101).[3] Indeed, many of the ideas of the *Manifesto* have been disseminated throughout the contemporary Italian theatre, as Italy's most prominent directors and actors (with the notable exception of Strehler) have consulted it as a source when confronting Pasolini's plays.[4] Nevertheless, the *Manifesto* itself is something of an uneven bit of writing, sometimes quite vague, at other times quite specific, and often enigmatic.

Pasolini begins his *Manifesto* with a discussion of audience, keenly aware that the intended audience determines the nature of an art work. Realizing that the modern theatre audience was almost solely bourgeois, he aimed at a select group of this already existing audience. He writes, "By *advanced groups of the bourgeoisie* we mean those few thousand intellectuals in every city whose cultural interest may be perhaps naive and provincial but nevertheless *real* . . . constituted for the most part by those who define themselves as 'left-wing progressives'" (*Manifesto* 133). Despite this reference to "left-wing progressives," he specifically states that his is not a party-line theatre. The chief criterion for determining his audience was not their political affiliation, but a genuine cultural interest, in accord with his desire that his theatre be a cultural rite. With this idea in mind, he wished to discard that part of the bourgeois audience which attended the theatre only as a social rite, as a social event. To discourage this portion of the bourgeois audience, he threatens, "A lady who attends the urban theatres and never misses a major Strehler, Visconti or Zeffirelli premiere . . . will have to pay thirty times the price of a normal ticket" (*Manifesto* 145).

In attempting to limit his audience Pasolini was deliberately taking an approach which his role as film director addressing a mass audience had not permitted him. Pasolini considered the average filmgoer to be mentally passive, "a simple, almost illiterate man" (*Descrizioni* 181). Certainly the characters in his neo-realist novels who attend the cinema are of this sort.[5] In contrast, he argued that his elitist approach to the theatre paradoxically allowed him to take what he termed "democratic" aims, as his theatre audience was to be mentally active, functioning as his equals. His theatre proposed "an exchange of ideas, a literary and political struggle in the most democratic . . . manner possible" (*Manifesto* 139). Such a symbiotic relationship between playwright and audience liberated him from what he perceived to be his more truly autocratic role as a director in the mass medium of film. He comments:

> In fact it is silly to confuse "democratic culture" with "mass culture." The "theatre of the Word" . . . is totally opposed to mass culture which is terrorist, repressive, stereotyped, un-human . . . certainly anti-democratic. Theatre . . . can never be a "mass medium": because theatre is not reproducible, only repeatable. (qtd. in Friedrich 104)

For Pasolini mass culture was quite distinct from popular or folk culture, which was generated directly by the people themselves. Instead, mass culture is a product marketed to the masses that confirms them in their role in capitalist society as lower class consumers. The producers and the consumers of mass culture are not one and the same, and the relationship between them is hierarchical.

Far from precluding social and political engagement, the elitism of Pasolini's theatre is intended as a means of furthering its social and political effectiveness. He contends:

> The theatre of the word . . . is the only one that can realistically reach the working class. *This class is in fact directly linked in a rapport with the advanced intellectuals.* This is a traditional notion, one inalienable from Marxist ideology and one which even the heretics and the orthodox cannot help but agree upon. (*Manifesto* 136)

Pasolini relics upon his advanced groups of bourgeois intellectuals to champion the working class, to play the role Lenin played in the Russian Revolution, a role which Pasolini himself ironically undercuts in the character of Pablo in *Calderón*. Oddly, although the relationship between author and his audience may be democratic, the relationship between the intellectuals that comprise this audience and the workers they champion is itself hierarchical. However, Pasolini saw such an approach as the only viable method of effecting a revolution. As early as 1960, in *The Dream of a Thing*, he had already come to satirize those who hoped to bring about revolution by naively confrontational means.

De Santi claims, "The democratic exercise that Pasolini speaks about in the *Manifesto* is the use of reason" (87). Pasolini's theatre follows in the Italian tradition of dialectical theatre in that its primary appeal is ostensibly to the intellect rather than to the emotions. Pasolini uses reason because he is addressing a select group of the bourgeoisie, that social class which flourished by making reason its religion, using it to reduce the universe to its own dimensions. This does not mean that he himself had recanted the scorn for reason which inspired much of his poetry and many of his films. As with elitism, it was merely a means to an end. De Santi concedes, "Reason is valued only as a means of consciously struggling against an old order" (89). As this old order was itself constructed on reason, Pasolini is, in effect, attempting to fight fire with fire, reason with reason. Responding to the student rebellions of the late 1960s, Pasolini admonished that "one cannot conduct an intelligent struggle against an enemy who is thought to be irreparably stupid" (*Descrizioni* 216). In accord with this belief, Pasolini's theatre constitutes probably his most sophisticated attempt to realize a revolution, as he astutely addresses himself to the powerful bourgeoisie rather than to the have-nots.

The theory of the "democratic" nature of Pasolini's theatre should be interpreted in light of the Italian semiologist Umberto Eco's concept of the "open" work, as Pasolini was familiar with Eco's theories and was influenced by them.[6] Eco views a work of art as a system of signs. Artistic form is no longer organic, but systematic in nature. In an "open" work the significance of this system of signs is not rigidly fixed by the creator of the work. Instead, there is an emphasis on the participation of the receiver of the work in determining and establishing the work's significance. This level of participation goes beyond the traditional role of interpretation so that the receiver, in a sense, actually contributes to the creation of the work of art for himself. The receiver literally constructs the work of art in his own mind based upon the signs the artist has given him. For Pasolini the theatrical event is a democratic process because he wants his audience to contribute as much to it as he does. In this sense, his spectators do become his equals, as their use of reason is integral in the construction of the theatrical event. Pasolini underscores the advanced intellectual nature of his intended audience by making esoteric allusions in his texts to a vast array of writers, even specifically recommending that his audience read certain relatively inaccessible linguists, theorists and political philosophers.

Of course, no work of art can be completely "open," as this would result in chaotic meaninglessness. Connotation cannot exist without being anchored to denotation at some point. Eco notes, "The *possibilities* which the work's openness makes available always work within a given *field of relations*" (*Role* 62). So-called open works are merely those in which there is a relatively wider field of relations. Meaning runs along a continuum from incomprehensibility, or what Eco calls "noise," to self-evident tautology. Pasolini's texts knowingly play upon the entire length of this continuum. Although seeming non sequiturs occur with a fair degree of frequency in the texts, the plays are just as likely to gravitate toward the self-reflective. When ambiguity is present, it is often systematic, directed. In *Calderón*, Pasolini states that his desire was "to give to ambiguity the form of absoluteness" (41). As ambiguity becomes absolute, or fixed, it transforms into paradox.

Groppali responds to the paradoxical nature of Pasolini's writing, asserting that the plays actually aspire to "the delirium of reason" ("Dalla realtà" 19). Indeed, such a phrase is an apt description of the combination of fatalistic logic and myth-like mystery to be found both in the plays and in his films of the period (*Teorema, Medea, Oedipus the King*). As the characters in these works take refuge in delirium, they become rational. As they take refuge in reason, they become delirious. In this manner Pasolini attempts to demonstrate the impotence of reason, its failure truly to reduce and/or absorb all that it encounters. In this context, the paradoxical nature of his plays can be viewed as an attempt at paralyzing the very same use of reason which the texts, as "open" works, require in order to be understood. Paradox would thus function for Pasolini as a means of eluding his audience on the continuum of signification. Having at once both employed and paralyzed his audience's use of reason, the significance of the sign systems of his plays must then ultimately be "felt."

Accordingly, Groppali has argued that Pasolini's is essentially a religious theatre. However, as such, it is not internally oriented as is the theatre of Grotowski. In contrast, the religious nature of Pasolini's theatre does not preclude his goal of creating a politically engaged theatre. Instead, he aspires to a fusion of the "religious rite" of Dionysian theatre and the "political rite" of the classical Greek theatre of Athens. He had found this fusion in Aeschylus' treatment of the religious myth of the *Oresteia*. He argues, "There is an exclusively single meaning to Orestes' tragedy—political" ("Introduzione," *Orestiade* 2). Pasolini attempts to reveal the political ramifications of religious archetypal myth, something which he does with perhaps more success in the plays *Pylades* and *Affabulation* than in his myth-inspired films of the period, *Medea* and *Oedipus the King*.

Dionysian theatre was religious inasmuch as it involved the ritual sacrifice of the old god, who was, in turn, replaced by a new, young god. In the classical theatre of Athens this rite became political, as plays focused on the replacement of one king, regime or dynasty with another. In accordance with this rite of kings, Oedipus kills Laius, only to be dethroned by Creon and his new order. In the *Oresteia*, Aegisthus kills Agamemnon and is, in turn, killed by Orestes. Essentially, Pasolini's theatre is about this rite of kings, this change of order, and how it has been upset in the modern bourgeois world. Although he does not explicitly address the topic of the Oedipal implications of the rite of kings in his *Manifesto*, this theme, in various guises, permeates virtually all his artistic output, including his films, novels and poetry. In his theatre he focuses upon the Oedipus-Laius tension in this rite, to the extent that the Jocasta role either becomes secondary or is neglected altogether. Pasolini's homosexuality thus comes to the fore in his theatre as it never did in his cinema. In any case, since this rite of kings is at the center of his dramatic output, it merits some discussion.

The basic pattern of the Oedipal rite remained largely intact from classical Greek tragedy to the romances of the medieval period. Tristan replaces King Mark at the side of Isolde, Robin Hood successfully challenges the authority of the sheriff of Nottingham, and Paolo takes the place of his older brother, Gianciotto, in the affections of Francesca da Rimini. Youth replaces age. The new order replaces the old order.

However, this rite of the succession of order was upset during the Renaissance, as the bourgeoisie came to power by means of the new secularism, a secularism which brought with it the disintegration of the Great Chain of Being. Political order was no longer believed to be contingent upon religious concepts and the divine right of kings was discarded in favor of government by social contract. This separation of church and state terminated the linear progression of systems of order. The result was a universe with "all coherence gone," a void in which the bourgeoisie constructed its own closed, finite power system. Consequently, as power became social rather than religious in nature, the bourgeoisie thrived.

The rise of the bourgeoisie contributed to both the precariousness and the perversion of the rite of kings which can be found in Renaissance drama. In Shakespeare, Macbeth kills Banquo, Brutus kills Caesar and Bolingbroke dethrones Richard II, but all three of these plays are characterized by an acute nostalgia for the order which has gone before. In *Macbeth* and *Julius Caesar* this nostalgia is so great that neither of the protagonists of these two plays successfully manages to establish a new order. In *Richard III* the Oedipal-Dionysian rite is so perverted that Richard does not, like Orestes, kill his uncle; he kills his nephews instead. Pasolini dates the theatre as a social rite back to this specific period. He writes, "The bourgeoisie . . . created . . . with Elizabethan theatre and the theatre of the Golden Age of Spain, and reaching to our times . . . a realistic, ironic, adventurous . . . SOCIAL RITE" (*Manifesto* 143). Interestingly, as a social phenomenon of the capitalistic bourgeoisie, the Elizabethan theatre was the first theatre in history to charge admission to its performances.

The bourgeois theatre has continued to flourish as a social rite promoting social roles only by detaching itself from both feudal and ancient conceptions of man's place in the universe. These earlier conceptions were basically in accord with Dionysian rite, which celebrated beauty, youth, strength and virility. Interestingly, these are also the same qualities generally prized by modern homosexual society. However, capitalist bourgeois society as a whole has established other criteria for determining power and a system of order, namely financial worth and the sociopolitical clout which usually accompanies it. Inasmuch as youth usually does not meet these criteria, bourgeois society and its theatre have inverted the rite of kings. The Oedipus figure fails to offer a viable new order and the old order of the Laius figure triumphs. In the serious drama of this century, Willy Loman smothers his sons' chances for success with his petit-bourgeois capitalist rhetoric in *Death of a Salesman*. In *Long Day's Journey into Night*, Tyrone's sense of self-importance has a similar effect on his sons.

However, in contrast to Miller and O'Neill, Pasolini takes a much more conscious and deliberate approach as he attempts to diagnose to what degree modern society has perverted the natural order. In *Affabulation* the Father actually and purposely kills his son. Pasolini's theatre is distinctive in that it focuses on the death of the prince, the neutralization of the Oedipus figure, which makes the triumph of the bourgeoisie inevitable. De Santi comments that "the bourgeoisie is incomplete without the degenerate son who screams his revolt" (82). The Oedipus figure may remain in the bourgeois theatre, but at best he has deteriorated into this degenerate son, and the seemingly new order he champions actually serves only to inadvertently promote the old order already in existence.

Because all of Pasolini's plays sustain this thesis, his theatre has been censured by leftist critics for pessimism. Nevertheless, the death or neutralization of the prince, evident in all his filmography from the death of Accattone to the elimination of the young victims in *Salò*, is at the very heart of his dramatic works. Pablo's illusions of revolution dissipate before the reductive reason of the older and more powerful bourgeois Basilio in *Calderón*. In *Orgy*, the Man, a product of bourgeois conformism and consumerism, claims to have killed both his sons. In *Pigsty* (1979; *Porcile*), Julian commits a ritual suicide while his father is involved in a nefarious business merger that will guarantee the prosperity of his industries. In *Pylades*, Pylades' dreams of revolution are shown to be both ineffectual and unwanted. In every case the prince must die, be neutralized or absorbed, because it is his agenda to bring a new order, to bring revolution.

However, the bourgeoisie reintegrates any threat of revolution into itself, even finding it profitable and marketing it as a consumer product. Consequently, any semblance of revolution is illusory and real revolution is impossible. The bourgeoisie remains self-perpetuating and its universe closed. The plays presuppose this closed universe, confronting what Ferretti calls "a petrified situation" (294). In a closed universe all action, whether Newtonian (based on physical movement) or Stanislavskian (based on psychological movement), would become illusory. Aristotle asserted that tragedy is the imitation of an action, but if action itself is illusory, the very existence of tragedy becomes dubious. In place of tragedy, the bourgeois theatre has established a "realistic, ironic, adventurous" dramatic tradition, using circumspection and reason to reduce tragedy to black comedy, melodrama, grotesque and tragicomedy. As Pasolini eschews this tradition, he proposes a paradoxical resolution to the problem of modern tragedy. The critic Viola Lou Canali observes, "Of all the attempts that have been made to come close to a modern tragedy, Pasolini's remains the only one that is truly modern. . . . He . . . has discovered that the tragedy of the bourgeoisie consists precisely in its inability to be tragic" (51).

De Santi criticizes this inability of the plays to be "tragic" in the classic sense. He writes, "The catatonia of the schemata renders the event insignificant and blocks the possibility of any confrontation" (81). However, the plays have a "catatonic schemata" precisely because Pasolini intended them as a reflection of bourgeois society, a more conscious and accurate reflection of that society and its condition than that offered by more standard commercial fare. If the events of his plays seem insignificant it is because they are purposely and consciously subjected to the same reductive use of reason which is so integral to the power structure of the bourgeoisie.

In fact, Pasolini's plays are not as static as De Santi would lead one to believe. Pasolini does not reject confrontation, but since his plays assume a closed universe, all confrontation must be directed inward. Consequently, the primary conflict in each of the plays is man versus himself. Accordingly, the plays are constructed largely out of the self-analyzing monologues of his characters. The critic Guido Santato describes Pasolini's theatre as "a drama of scission, of the intimate contradictions which propose themselves in the form of a liberating psychodrama on the stage" (268). The characters are virtually bereft of the usual defense mechanisms of the unconscious, so that the plays examine the exposed divided self. The bourgeois in his social Laius-role must confront his more natural identity, the Oedipus-role origins which he has denied. Because his universe is closed, his divided self cannot be transcended. It can only be negated, either by allowing a social role to usurp totally the individual's identity, or else by suicide. Carotenuto observes, "Death . . . continually returns to ratify the inevitability of an existentially degraded condition" (20). This "existentially degraded condition" is the fall of man, a fall which the bourgeoisie has perpetuated by separating the world political order from the spiritual universal order so that it could come to power.

Pasolini uses this fall as the basis for his aesthetic in formulating his theories for the theatre of the word. His seminal work *Heretical Empiricism* (1972; *Empirismo Eretico*) serves to fill in many of the blanks Pasolini left empty by his *Manifesto*, as it contains a far more fully articulated explanation of the fall as it manifests itself in the phenomenon of language. He writes, "The purest form of language that exists in the world, the only one which can be called simply LANGUAGE and nothing else, is the language of natural reality itself. . . . Reality does nothing else but talk to itself using human experience as its vehicle" (*Empirismo* 254). Another passage reads: "What does a 'signifier' do regarding 'the signified': it 'signifies' it? This is a tautology. . . . In reality there is no 'signified': because the signified is also a signifier . . . certainly not a written-spoken signifier, but an iconic-living one" (*Empirismo* 268). For Pasolini there is no Edenic language which can be reduced to an elemental binary correlation between signifier and signified. Signs can signify only other signs and never a representamen, because in every case the indicated representamen is just another sign. Signs can signify only other signs and never a representamen, because in every case the indicated representamen is only another sign. Lacan has asserted that "no signification can exist without reference to another signifier" (150). In such a system meaning can only "insist" through metaphor rather than "consist" in declaration. For Pasolini, the perceptible fallen universe becomes a metaphor of its original, pre-fallen self. He describes a universe in which everything is removed from itself, and implicit within this removal is the fact that things do not simply exist but are also expressive of themselves. Accordingly, he refers to "the book of the world, the book of nature, the prose of practice, the poetry of life" (*Empirismo* 267). Traditional semiotics allows for the possibility of unintentional signification (e.g., natural phenomena such as earthquakes and volcanic eruptions, and gestures, signs and even words employed by accident). Rejecting this concept, Pasolini asserted that there can be no accident. For him, there was always an intention, a meaning, on some level, even in natural phenomena, as he considered all the world to be a language, a code. He called for the formulation of a semiology of all reality, an idea which prompted Eco to accuse him of "singular semiotic naiveté" (qtd. in Zigaina 275).

Actually, Pasolini's "semiotic naiveté" is not entirely dissimilar from the psychosemiological theories of Lacan, as for both, expressiveness and the very process of signification itself is contingent upon and implicit in a fall and a dissolution of wholeness. From such a perspective, meaning is assumed to be essentially diacritical in nature, resulting from a separation of elements that renders them distinguishable, a separation of elements which wholeness precludes. Lacan labels the principle of signification the "Law of the Father." As with narcissism (see chapter 1), this "Law" evolves in response to the fall from the wholeness of the symbiotic mother-infant relationship, intruding upon this relationship and hastening its disintegration. As this disintegration leaves the infant with a sense of lack and a concomitant sense of desire,

Lacan has asserted that the moment "in which desire becomes human is also that in which the child is born into language" (103). The mother-infant symbiosis corresponds to Pasolini's androgynous original God and His pre-fallen universe, while the Lacanian "Law of the Father" recalls Pasolini's authoritarian Laius-like God of the fall.

In ordering the universe and rendering it intelligible, the "Law of the Father" performs a rational function, and Pasolini's own disdain for reason comes to mind. However, Pasolini's concept of the word remains distinct from Lacan's "Law," owing more instead to Lacan's concept of the phallus-signifier. Although the advent of the phallus and its accompanying absence-of-phallus constitutes the diacritical splitting of the androgynous whole into individual genders, Lacan conceived of it as the symbol of symbology itself, as "the signifier of signifiers." As such, the phallus-signifier is a metasymbol and a metasignifier that relates to the metalinguistic nature of Pasolini's theatre. For Lacan, this phallus-signifier was the place where the inexpressible becomes expressible, or, to adopt Groppali's terminology, where delirium and reason coalesce. Inasmuch as the Lacanian phallus and the Pasolinian word are one, Pasolini's dedication of his theatre to the word prompts him to devote a number of passages in the plays to the phallus both as symbol (hence Pasolini's concern for transcending the rational-irrational dialectic) and as anatomical organ (hence the recurrent theme of homosexuality as vehicle for this transcendence).

The critic Marco Vallora extrapolates on the implications of the fall and the resultant expressiveness of "the Law of the Father" for Pasolini's aesthetics. He comments on Pasolini's peculiar semiotic approach: "In short, nature has already become artifice, culture, spectacle; nothing of the primary, the elementary exists any longer; every remnant is a preexistent code, art descends into life . . . reality tends to become art, or better yet, it already is art" ("Metaletteratura," in Roncaglia 120). Such an aesthetic can be viewed as merely a natural extension of Pasolini's earlier neo-realism. In his neo-realist films he had cast boys from the subproletariat as boys from the subproletariat. He had cast Orson Welles as a film director, Enzo Siciliano as a critic and himself as a writer. The casts in his films were at once themselves and at the same time cinematic images, or signs, of themselves. Vallora describes Pasolini's neo-realism: "In short . . . reality writes itself immediately on the film without mediation" (129). There is no need for mediation or manipulation, as reality is inherently expressive already.

For Pasolini, it was not the artist's function to create, but to reveal the expressiveness already inherently within the code of the world, to reveal the preexistence of art within the very fabric of reality. The work of art becomes a pastiche of the art of the world. In this context, the influence on Pasolini of the Italian writer of pastiche, Carlo Emilio Gadda, should not be neglected. Pasolini's senior by a generation, Gadda was one of the few writers whom Pasolini venerated. He admired Gadda's *That Awful Mess on the Via Merulana* (1958; *Quer pasticciaccio brutto de Via Merulana*) in particular. The critic Olga Ragusa's comments on the pastiche form of the novel reveal its underlying relationship to Eco's concept of the "open" work. She writes, "In *Quer pasticciaccio*, though the reader is never directly addressed, he is constantly drawn into the story as a participant. Over and over again, the pieces of the puzzle are left in his hands and he is left to do with them what he can" ("Gadda," in Pacifici 249–50).

Gadda appropriated the language of the world, its various signs and semantic structures, as givens to be used as elements to be orchestrated in his work. Pasolini elaborates upon this tradition in a typically post-modernist way, appropriating not only the signs of the world, but also the established iconography and ideology of other writers and artists, as well as that of his own earlier works.[7] Zigaina, Vallora and Santato have all viewed Pasolini as a mannerist who primarily embroidered upon already existing materials and principles. The leftist critic Franco Fortini observes:

> Pasolini discovers the limitless stylistic possibilities of the pastiche, of the imaginary translation, of the "copy," and with absolute seriousness and detachment, exploiting his extraordinary "manneristic" qualities . . . he creates a series of works "through" which rather than "in" which he succeeds in giving concrete poetic representations. . . . They are never "sources," but schemes, pretexts, supporting evidence, in a word, contaminations. (qtd. in Zigaina 273)

Pasolini himself claimed, "I work under the sign of contamination" (qtd. in Zigaina 274). Pasolini cannot create an original, because for him nothing of the original exists any longer in the world. He can only contaminate his givens and recombine his fragmentary *corps morcelé* in such a way as to reveal their already inherent expressiveness. Zigaina terms this process a "jump" (Italian: *salto*). Although this "jump" may call to mind the "transcendence" of Romantic aesthetics, in post-modernism the process is perhaps more intellectual than inspirational.

If all the world is expressive, if reality is already a language, then traditional spoken and written language becomes metalingual. Pasolini calls this language "the first social contract." It is a product of society, indicative of man's fall from grace. Words become symptomatic of the divided self, as they can signify and express something other than themselves, much as man adopts social roles that are removed from his original self. Interpreting Pasolini's theory in a Lacanian manner, Roncaglia comments, "The word manifests itself as compensation for a privation of being. . . . The word and, therefore, poetry are creations of man inasmuch as he is an 'imperfect animal'" (19). Language, like bourgeois society, is seen as an artificial construct, the product neither of man's animal nature nor his spiritual nature, but of his intellect, his rational processes, his consciousness. Pasolini associates language at the metalingual level specifically with the bourgeoisie. He notes, "A constant and important metalinguistic consciousness exists only in the heart of the bourgeoisie" (*Empirismo* 267). He can make use of such metalingual consciousness in his plays only because he specifically sets out to address the more advanced groups of the bourgeoisie.

In a closed universe, fallen from its original state, this metalinguistic system of signs created by the bourgeoisie risks becoming as hermetic and arbitrary as the system of power established by this social class. Lacan referred to the "sliding" of the signified beneath the signifier, but the French semiologist Roland Barthes argues, "The fact is that there is absolutely no parallelism between reality and language" (qtd. in Roncaglia 117). As the word becomes disengaged from reality, any significance which may be gleaned from its relationship to other signs (i.e., words) in the system becomes precarious. The metaphoric "insistence" of meaning is jeopardized by the "absoluteness" of the detachment of the signifier from the signified. Words become abstract and functionally obsolete. Pasolini writes, "I am familiar with, and by now *want* the uselessness of every word" ("Il Gracco," *Le poesie* 601). He admits:

> Expression detached from things,
> signs made music . . .
> . . . I would like . . .
> . . . to compose music
> perhaps the only expressive act
> which is as high and indefinable
> as the actions of reality.
>
> ("Ceneri" 25–26)

By writing in verse, Pasolini attempted to emphasize the musicality of words, to purify them, to underscore their abstractness. On the one hand, he uses words as signifiers to construct arguments and stimulate debate as part of the democratic process of his theatre. On the other hand, he seems to believe that these arguments and debates are essentially and irrevocably disengaged from the realities they ostensibly address. In fact, his plays illustrate, or as Barthes would say, "demonstrate," in both their structure and use of language, the reality of this disengagement. Consequently, Pasolini's theatre constitutes a sometimes uneasy, sometimes fascinating synthesis of the two Italian traditions of literary hermeticism and neo-realist social engagement.

4

Calderón

Calderón became the first of Pasolini's plays to be published in book form in 1973 and remained the only one of his plays to be so published during his lifetime. The critical reception of the text was somewhat mixed. However, Pasolini himself asserted, "I am certain that *Calderón* is one of my surest formal successes" (*Descrizioni* 213). Indeed, the play is well-structured, highly formalized, even crystalline, not unlike what Pasolini called "the Chinese box" structure of his film *A Thousand and One Nights*. This structure results from Pasolini's desire to explore the ambiguous nature of reality and identity. Following in the Pirandellian tradition, *Calderón* is composed of various levels of represented reality. However, Pasolini's play goes even further, exploring not only reality within reality, but dream within dream. Reality and identity are contingent upon not only a social context but also a Jungian one. In addition, the various levels of reality undercut one another, creating a sort of *Verfremdungseffekt* which allows Pasolini a sense of critical distance. The play thus extends from the surrealistic to the Brechtian.

Calderón is divided into twenty-six episodes, or scenes, and three interludes. The interludes constitute the level of reality farthest removed from the action of the plot. In them, the Speaker addresses the audience directly, discussing matters of an aesthetic nature involving the production itself. The play, a bourgeois document, thus self-consciously comments upon itself as a play. The play functions most fully in a Brechtian manner on the next level, which, although removed from the dramatic action as well, comments on this action. In these scenes, King Basilio and Queen Lupe also address the audience directly, but as characters rather than as Pasolini's mouthpiece. They do not address themselves to aesthetic concerns, but to the philosophical and political significance which may be gleaned from the plot.

The next level is the more traditional level of the dramatic action itself. The play begins when Rosaura, the protagonist, awakens to a world she does not recognize. She finds herself as a daughter in a wealthy bourgeois family in Madrid. She meets Sigismondo, who was her mother's lover before her mother married. Rosaura falls in love with Sigismondo only to discover he is her real father. She then awakens to find herself a prostitute in a shantytown on the outskirts of Barcelona. A boy, Pablo, is ushered into her shack by his friends. Instead of making love, he woos her with his philosophical and revolutionary talk. She falls in love with him only to discover he is her son, the son whom she believed to have died in infancy and whom her sister and mother sold. When she awakens the third time, her name is no longer Rosaura, but Maria Rosa, and she is a mother in a petit-bourgeois family, married to Basilio. She denies her role even more adamantly than before, to the point where she is institutionalized in a mental hospital. When she recovers, she returns home. Student riots are in progress outside, and one of the students involved, Pablo, comes in seeking refuge from the police. When Basilio begins a diatribe, Maria Rosa and Pablo fall asleep. When she reawakens the fourth time, it is to her ostensibly "real" world, as she realizes that her nightmarish life actually transpires in a Nazi prison camp *lager*.

Rosaura's three dreams and fourth "reality" function as Pasolini's contamination of the traditional dramatic form of three acts and an epilogue. The Speaker asserts that the play "is not intended as nostalgia for the old theatre, but adopts the old theatre . . . as an expressive element of uncertain meaning" (*Calderón* 171). However, with *Calderón*, Pasolini does not merely contaminate dramatic form in general, but two original works of art in particular, specifically Calderón de la Barca's *Life Is a Dream* and Diego Velazquez' *Las Meniñas*.[1] Thematically, *Calderón* is more akin to *Life Is a Dream*, as Pasolini and Calderón share an interest in the ambiguous nature of reality and identity, the death (albeit symbolic) of the prince, and the limitations of love in overcoming the barriers of power. However, structurally, Pasolini's play is probably more reminiscent of *Las Meniñas*. The critic Cesare Musati writes that "the ambient of the painting also includes the space in which we find ourselves, and so we feel ourselves paradoxically within the painting at the same time" (55). Similarly, Velazquez himself appears in the painting, which, like Pasolini's script, is a play of mirrors directed both outward and inward. The levels of the Speaker and of King Basilio and Queen Lupe are directed outward toward the audience in an attempt to include the audience within the play. These levels also represent Pasolini himself, his critical stance, as he remains within the play but not within the fiction of the dramatic action, in much the same position where Velazquez envisioned himself in *Las Meniñas*.

Pasolini can also be found within his play on the level of the universal Jungian unconscious, the level where his creative process and the actions of his characters meet. This is the level that reflects inward from the dramatic action. Manacorda comments on *Calderón*, "It seems to me to be the text wherein Marx has been abandoned in the name of Jung or Freud" (81). In fact, the level of the dramatic action is continually undermined by the unconscious of Rosaura, and is seen in retrospect as a mere projection of that unconscious. She insists that her reality is a dream and her dream is a reality. The self is at one with the world of the dream because the dreamworld is a projection of the self. The world of the dream is a fully integrated world, a unified whole which precludes any anarchic or hierarchic power structure. Inasmuch as man creates the world of his dream, he is like a god; inasmuch as his libido is uninhibited in the dream by the socializing forces of the conscious, he is like an animal. His divine and animal natures are unified and sublimated in his dream.

Basilio comments on the sleeping Maria Rosa and Pablo:

> Having abandoned themselves to the sleep of the innocent
> . . . And I am awake, the husband alone,
> rendered a cuckold by sleep. . . .
> it is easy for you, student, to give lessons in purity,
> and with nothing other than your very existence.
>
> (*Calderón* 166)

Pablo and Maria Rosa can make love in their dreams, as they never could while awake. Basilio continues, referring to Pablo's erection:

> With that antenna raised to the world
> you indicate, like a young animal,
> the area of the woods where you are master
> and nothing can contradict this sign.
>
> (*Calderón* 167)

In sleep, man recovers his pre-fallen state; he is "innocent" and can give "lessons in purity." In contrast, the bourgeois Basilio finds his identity solely within the conscious state, refusing to relinquish his conscious use of reason. As a bourgeois, his power is contingent upon his fallen state; the unconscious renders him impotent and makes him a cuckold.

Mental illness is analogous to the dream state in that both permit an abdication of an identity which is artificially imposed by a social context. Like the dreamer, the mentally ill person creates a world which is at one with himself, rather than modifying himself to a world which is external and ultimately superfluous to him. Instead of alienating the self, he alienates his social context. The doctor Manuel, who treats Maria Rosa at the mental hospital, defends the mentally ill:

> After all, they have the courage
> to give into a feeling which devalues
> a life that deserves to be devalued:
> and they've been capable of accomplishing this enormity.
>
> (*Calderón* 148)

Although dreams are of thematic importance in all six of the plays, *Calderón* is the one conceived as if in a dream. However, Pasolini's interest in unconscious states did not begin with *Calderón*. It pervades much of his Friulan verse and can be found in many of his films, even the neo-realistic *Accattone*. The elimination of the victims in *Salò*, the flight of the birds in *A Thousand and One Nights*, Giotto's vision of the Madonna in *The Decameron*, and the entirety of *Teorema* are all dominated and even determined by a sense of dream logic, of dreamlikeness. Pasolini called this surrational quality "onoricity" (Italian: *onoricità*). In the above-mentioned film sequences, he attempts to renounce overtly conscious control, encouraging the artistic structures to evolve on their own, just as the dreamer is not in control of the dreamworld he creates. Consequently, there is a direct relationship between Pasolini's interest in the dream state and the hermeticism of his art. Barthes has asserted that "it is language which speaks, not the author; to write is, through an impersonality (not at all to be confused with the castrating objectivity of the realist novelist), to reach that point where only language acts, 'performs' and not 'me'" (*Image* 143). This is certainly the effect Pasolini achieves in *Calderón*, as verbal images and passages of dialogue are repeated, superimposed, placed within new contexts, and spoken by different characters, from scene to scene. In this manner, language acts so that the meaning of Pasolini's imagery is expanded upon, contaminated, given added dimension. As a result, in addition to its intertextual indebtedness to *Life Is a Dream* and *Las Meniñas*, the play develops an intratextual relationship with itself, building upon itself. In the process, Pasolini as a writing persona becomes transparent, disappearing into the very fabric of his work, much as the persona of Velazquez remains indistinct from the composition of his painting.

The hermetic nature of *Calderón* undermines any Newtonian concept of time, as Pasolini embraces Freud's theory that time does not exist in the unconscious workings of the psyche. In the fully integrated world of the dreamer, there is no separation of elements, there is no separation of time. As power cannot be hierarchical in the dream state, time cannot be chronological. As the play rejects an empirical concept of the universe, it also negates the possibility of empirical action. Consequently, as a hermetic construct, *Calderón* replaces the Aristotelian climax, which is based on such action, with what Manacorda calls "beauty as the cathartic moment in the story" (82). Similarly, Pasolini claims that the play was written "partly due to philosophic literary narcissism" (qtd. in *Il Tempo* 28 March 1980). As in Jackson Pollack's Abstract Expressionism, the act of expression itself is expressive. The signifier becomes itself the signified. In a Barthesian manner, the play attempts to demonstrate the formation of a system of signs in a process analogous to the dream process itself, rather than using this system of signs to represent something else, as in the traditional theatre. As such, *Calderón* is where Barthes and Freud meet.

Lacan claimed that the individual was "born into language," that he was thrown into a pre-established discourse in an almost Kafkaesque manner. Lacan asserted that "the truth of his history is not all contained in his script" (155). The life of the individual is actually a larger script in which he may "know only his own lines." Certainly Rosaura experiences just such a sensation in her repeated awakenings. In the first two sequences, she awakens screaming, a technique Pasolini was to use in *Beast of Style* and *Affabulation* as well. In essence, waking from the dream state constitutes a birth trauma that is existential in nature. The unity of the self and the world which characterizes the dream state is severed upon waking, as the waking world is outside the self rather than within the self. The psychic order inherent within the dream is dispelled: man must either confront the void around him or take refuge within the social order of the bourgeoisie. Rinaldi notes, "To adapt, as always, means to lose truth. To learn to speak according to reality means to renounce the knowledge of the profound, to lose oneself" (309). Instead, Rosaura wants to retain herself, to maintain a sort of psychic integrity. To this end, she denies her external world and resists the identities it attempts to impose upon her. The alternative of accepting her social roles would entail the alienation of her original, pre-fallen self. Sigismondo describes the condition, "I will continue to run along a track parallel / to that along which my life should have run" (*Calderón* 31). This sense of being outside oneself pervades and torments Pasolini's characters, much as it had Pirandello's.

In contrast to Rosaura, her sister and Basilio willingly change their roles according to their social context. Basilio is a king in the first sequence and a self-proclaimed bourgeois in the third sequence. He admonishes her, "Recognize your life in that of others / Rosaura, and you will see that it will be REAL" (*Calderón* 40). He maintains that reality is essentially objective, that there is no original self, no prime matter to the self, that the self is defined solely from within the context of external reality. Rosaura's sister's identity is so contingent upon this external social context that her name alternates from sequence to sequence, changing from Stella to Carmen to Agostina. Naturally, she is also very insistent that Rosaura assume her social role as well.

However, Rosaura wants to return to her pre-conscious existence. In the third sequence, Agostina describes to her one of her recurrent dreams:

> Perhaps you have had one of your usual dreams . . .
> That of the falcon who flies over Spain
> above the vast dried and yellowed
> fields of summer,
> neatly parcelled along the brown roads,
> which lead from one town to another, each (as you say)
> in the form of a vulva. . . .
> He falls upon you, and with his beak he violates
> your mouth, inserting his small teeth of coral.
>
> (*Calderón* 136–37)

In an earlier passage, Sigismondo had also described the Spanish land as a vulva, the earth as mother. Rosaura's dream of the falcon calls to mind Freud's study of Da Vinci, wherein he examines Da Vinci's claim of having been violated by a bird in his infancy. The imagery is at once both sexual and ethereal, a fusion of man's animal and divine natures wherein his libido is sublimated rather than forced to confront the divided self of the birth trauma of the waking state. The beak as phallus, the coral teeth as semen, the falcon himself, all correspond to Freud's theory that dreams of flight express a desire to maintain orgasm, to transcend. The transcendence of flight cannot exist in the enclosed bourgeois universe of the action of *Calderón*, so Rosaura can find it only in the dream state. As Rosaura/Maria Rosa is forced to accept her bourgeois identity, she must discard her hopes of flight or transcendence. She responds to her fallen state in the third sequence, "The eagles have been back beneath the sidewalks for some time now" (*Calderón* 139).[2]

Flight imagery recurs throughout Pasolini's work, often within the context of dreams, and it is almost always representative of a sort of transcendence of man's fallen state. The flight of the servant Emilia in *Teorema* is proof of her spiritual being, her sainthood. The pianist in *Salò* hurls herself from a window, as the only means of liberating herself from the enclosed and artificial world established by the fascists in power. Accattone takes a symbolic flight in *Accattone*, a dive into the Tiber that permits him a Freudian return to the womb of the water below, a return to a pre-fallen state. Similarly, Riccetto must dive into the river in the novel *The Ragazzi* in order to rescue a swallow and release it into flight. In *A Thousand and One Nights* the dream of the flight of the birds becomes a leitmotif of the film. Such imagery can also be found in most of the plays.

Pasolini may concentrate on Freud and Jung in *Calderón*, but he does not abandon Marx completely. He sets his play in Franchist Spain because fascism rigidifies the artificially imposed sense of order perpetrated by the bourgeoisie, emphasizing its hierarchical rather than organic nature. The rigidity of the system of order in fascism attempts to compensate for its lack of truer unity. Queen Lupe declares in *Calderón*, "Where order reigns, there reigns unity. / And unity gives us the greatest of consolations" (39). This unity is a mere consolation because it is false and artificial, as the bourgeoisie has attempted to substitute the maxim "Where order reigns, there reigns unity" for its inverse, "Where unity reigns, there reigns order." For Pasolini unity implies order, but not vice-versa.

With the characters of Pablo and Sigismondo, Pasolini studies the possibility of effecting a revolution. To a certain extent, Pablo and Sigismondo are the same character. They are both the prince, the Oedipal projection of Pasolini's self. Insofar as they serve the same function, they never appear onstage at the same time, although both are at least mentioned in all three sequences. Sigismondo refers to himself as "a poet on the banks of the Duero. / My soul weighs heavy upon me" (*Calderón* 29). The Duero River in Spain here replaces Pasolini's own Tagliamento of the Friuli. Like Pasolini, Sigismondo flees the land of his youth and takes refuge in Rome. Basilio calls Sigismondo a "communist atheist" and a "reactionary," two criticisms often levelled at Pasolini by his adversaries. While Pasolini felt himself excluded from society because of his homosexuality, Sigismondo is excluded both as a Jew and as a political exile. Sigismondo is the biological father of Rosaura in the first sequence, and of Pablo in the second sequence, but in both cases he has been separated from his offspring so that he has not played the authoritarian Laius father role. Instead, he maintains his Oedipal prince identity. As a former Republican revolutionary who lost to Franco, he has never come to power and played the Laius role in the political sphere either.

The failure of Sigismondo's revolution foreshadows the failure of Pablo's. Pablo fashions himself as a classical Marxist intellectual who incites the oppressed to revolution. However, Pablo, like Pasolini, has been brought up in a bourgeois environment. His name "Pablo" is the Spanish equivalent of Pasolini's middle name "Paolo." Pablo frequents the slums of Barcelona much as Pasolini maintained an affinity for the subproletariat on the outskirts of Rome. The Andalusian inhabitants of the ghettoes of Barcelona function here as the counterparts of the southern Italian immigrants who came to Rome after World War II. Like Pasolini, Pablo is homosexual, but unlike Pasolini, Pablo values his homosexuality inasmuch as it helps save him from the bourgeois trap of social conformity. His hero is an imprisoned revolutionary named Velazquez. He tells Rosaura, "He is like Socrates with the Athenian boys" (*Calderón* 94). Velazquez thus reflects Pasolini's own dual role as homosexual and mentor of young revolutionaries.

Pablo proclaims his disregard for authority and his Oedipal identity, "We reject all fathers" (161). However, as a revolutionary in Franchist Spain in the late 1960s, he is something of an anomaly. He is, in fact, described as "one / who in this August of '67 looks more to Rome / than to Madrid" (*Calderón* 123). Basilio views Pablo as just another degenerate son of the bourgeoisie, a manifestation of its intestinal struggle. He calls Pablo "a political delinquent." Echoing Pasolini's own sentiments regarding the student rebellions in Rome, Pablo accepts Basilio's criticism, conceding that "a poor adolescent policeman / from the subproletariat of Andalusia / is politically purer than I" (*Calderón* 164–65). Basilio deflates Pablo's delusions of revolution when Pablo seeks refuge from the police in Basilio's bourgeois home. He coyly debates the issue with him:

> BASILIO: The workers weren't with you? . . .
> PABLO: We'll try to get closer to them in the future. . . .
> BASILIO: Do they want to be courted?
>
> (*Calderón* 160)

In effect, the revolutionary fails to represent the oppressed. Instead, his revolution expresses merely his own dissatisfaction with his bourgeois role, his reluctance to accept his Laius identity. Not wanting to confront either his bourgeois identity or Basilio's reductive use of reason, Pablo retreats into sleep. Basilio takes advantage of the situation, threatening to phone the police to hand Pablo over to them. Pablo's revolution has failed.

Basilio expounds upon his victory:

> Power is served by him who criticizes it.
> . . . Power has always
> recreated itself
> equal to itself
> . . . because
> no contestation of me is sincere.
>
> (*Calderón* 175–76)

Every ostensible revolution ultimately results in a power structure which, in the fallen universe, is unavoidably bourgeois. As Oedipus figures, Sigismondo and Pablo are merely would-be Laius figures. Rinaldi calls them "reformists whom the bourgeoisie sends ahead to renew itself from within" (311). Their Oedipus role is an illusion or, at best, only a temporary state. Their absorption into the bourgeoisie is as inevitable as the absorption of their revolutions. As Pablo and Sigismondo fail in their Oedipal roles, the play illustrates the recurrent theme of the death of the prince. The critic Gerardo Guerrieri views Calderón's *Life Is a Dream* as a clear predecessor of Pasolini's theatre in this regard. He observes that in Calderón's masterpiece "there is a father, King Basilio, who imprisons his son as soon as he is born: repression and oppression by the father, destruction to the sons." Similarly, Pasolini's Pablo and Sigismondo find themselves imprisoned in the enclosed universe of the bourgeoisie.

Pasolini clearly identifies Basilio as the Laius figure in the play. He notes, "Power in *Calderón* is called Basilio" (*Descrizioni* 214). Unlike Sigismondo, Basilio embraces his authoritarian father role, playing it not only with his children but also with his wife, calling her his "prodigal daughter" because of her retreat into irrational behavior. However, as a Laius figure, Basilio is an example of what Santato calls "the modern, democratic application of astutely permissive power" (283). Disclaiming fascism, Basilio is tolerant of both his father-in-law's communism and Pablo's revolutionary rhetoric. It is his bourgeois use of reason which allows him to adapt to changes in the dramatic situation and to assimilate all challenges to his authority. However, as the bourgeois attempts to be all-encompassing and all-absorbing, he suffers from a sort of paralysis. Like Hamlet, Basilio is usually left contemplating action rather than taking action. He is too wise to himself, knowing that in his closed universe all action is illusory anyway. However, in removing himself from the action, he is also removed from himself. He becomes a victim of the very same self-alienation and dissociation he uses to perpetuate and ensure his survival. In *Teorema*, *Orgy* and *Affabulation* Pasolini was to concentrate more fully on the bourgeoisie as a victim of itself.

Aware that every Oedipus is a would-be Laius and every challenge to the power of the bourgeoisie is insincere, Pasolini turns to Rosaura as his protagonist in order to escape the Oedipus-Laius polemic. Although female characters are not infrequent in Pasolini's work, female protagonists are relatively rare. Rosaura has only two female protagonist predecessors, Medea and Mamma Roma. Medea actually plays the Oedipus role, challenging Jason's Laius and his use of reason with her emphasis on and faith in the occult and the spiritual. Arguably more a creation of Anna Magnani than of Pasolini, Mamma Roma is nevertheless an incarnation of the ideal mother figure which can be found in *The Turks in Friuli* and *The Gospel according to Matthew*. The mother figure is of integral importance in Pasolini inasmuch as she represents a unity of the self with the world prior to birth trauma, a unity not unlike that found in the dream state. Groppali writes of "the sweet and chaste anti-inferno of the maternal womb" (*L'ossessione* 97). Pasolini stresses the importance of Rosaura's maternal nature, as she has maternal feelings for her younger brother in the first sequence and is a mother in the last two sequences. She follows her maternal instincts in wanting to retreat into the womb of her dreams rather than Oedipally trying to challenge and confront the power structure as do Pablo and Sigismondo. Unlike these two, Rosaura does not aspire to integration with society but with her self.

Consequently, she seeks a truer nonconformism and escape from social roles than that offered by the anticonformist conformism of Pablo and Sigismondo. Manuel describes her retreat from the world into mental illness in the third sequence:

> Thus Maria Rosa has found a way
> of disobeying without being disobedient
> and she will return to obey without being obedient.
>
> (*Calderón* 149)

This concept of detachment from the Oedipus-Laius polemic recurs throughout Pasolini's plays and the above phrase itself is of central importance in characterizing Julian in *Pigsty*. However, detachment, withdrawal and retreat from political action are themselves political actions. In seeking to transcend the bourgeoisie by turning inward to her own psyche, Rosaura becomes outwardly passive. Pablo attacks her sociopolitical passivity as tacit support of the bourgeois power structure. In the third sequence she is even on intimate terms with this power structure, as she is married to Basilio. In all three sequences she is a victim of her own passivity, as she is forced to awaken, to acquiesce to the power structure in which she finds herself, to take part in the pre-established discourse and to accept her social role. Pasolini condemns such passivity as complicity vehemently in *Salò*, wherein the youths, like Rosaura, have an intimate rapport with those in power. In *Calderón*, it is not so much Rosaura's youth as it is her status as a woman which determines her passivity and victimization. Pablo makes this explicit when he berates her, "You also accept your inferiority as a woman" (*Calderón* 100).

However, Rosaura's maternal instincts are not totally bereft of a solution to the dilemma of the closed universe of the bourgeoisie. Where Sigismondo and Pablo attempt to create an opening in this universe by means of revolution, Rosaura aims to transcend it by means of love. *Calderón* is unique among Pasolini's plays in that it is the only text in which he explores love in a Romantic manner as a means of integrating man's animal and divine natures. In his filmography, love successfully accomplishes such a transcendence only in *A Thousand and One Nights*, when the lovers are finally united in the end. In *Calderón*, when Rosaura can no longer manage to retreat into her dreamworld, she seeks love. Santato writes, "Even if the dream is finished, this does not necessarily mean that love must finish, just as in Calderón's *Life Is a Dream*" (283). Love supposedly transcends the arbitrary boundaries of dream and reality.

Accordingly, a sense of *voix du sang* permeates the play, as Rosaura is instinctively and inextricably attracted first to Sigismondo and then to Pablo, although she has no idea why. Sigismondo and Pablo reciprocate this attraction. Rosaura falls in love in both cases only to discover that her love is of an incestuous nature. Consequently, this path to transcendence leads her only to an impasse, so that the action of the play must abruptly stop and then begin again, as she wakes from another dream. The critic Roberto De Monticelli notes, "The failure is total in all three dreams. Love, the spark which should leap over the social cages, is a 'diverse' love, so much so as to violate ancient taboos" ("I tre sogni"). Another critic, Gennaro Aceto, views this failure of love as a reflection of Pasolini's own failure to find fulfillment in a homosexual relationship. He notes, "Pasolini adapts incest to his own inquietude, he transforms it into a grief-ridden autobiography, he translates it into the impossibility of loving."

Failing to provide a transcendence of the closed world of the bourgeoisie, love degenerates either into the bourgeois institution of marriage, or into base animality, or into, as has already been discussed, the Freudian imagery of dreams. Basilio reduces love to a social function wherein he, as Rosaura/Maria Rosa's husband, should supposedly sublimate her incestuous attraction to both her father Sigismondo and her son Pablo. He comments, "Love as conceived by us, the Bourgeois King, / is unthinkable without a social sense" (*Calderón* 39).

The love between Sigismondo and Doña Lupe, Rosaura's mother in the first sequence, was without this social sense. She could not marry him for social reasons—his race and his political ideology. Separated from Sigismondo during the Spanish Civil War, Doña Lupe learned to accept her role as a wealthy bourgeois and not to love him. If love constitutes the impulse for union and integration, then unrequited love merely serves as a reminder of alienation and a lack of wholeness. The trauma of failing to achieve a transcendence and/or integration transforms the love impulse into sadomasochism, as the need for union becomes increasingly more insistent and violent, a process Pasolini was to study in greater detail in *Salò* and *Orgy*. Sigismondo tells Rosaura of his love for Doña Lupe:

> Finding her so, I raped her.
> Yes, that which you think is in the sublime form
> of a pine cone, or a magnificent rose which opens in the morning,
> and with which the husband impregnates his wife with their blessed offspring
> I imposed upon your mother with hate and vengeance
> or with a love which no longer wanted to call itself such.
>
> (*Calderón* 67)

Man discards his divine nature in order to take blind refuge in his animal nature, thereby avoiding having to confront his divided self.

In the second sequence, the prostitute Rosaura has despaired of the possibility of divine love, and so turns to the animal side of her nature. When she is attracted to Pablo, she asks him bluntly, "How are you between the legs?" (*Calderón* 86). The play contains numerous references, both poetic and graphic, to genitalia. In a manner reminiscent of Rimbaud (an early influence on Pasolini), Pasolini virtually spiritualizes man's animal nature as a means of escaping the self-consciousness of social roles, bourgeois or otherwise. For Rosaura, her physical being is an expression of her spiritual being. She claims, "My body is sacred, it is with my body that I live" (*Calderón* 55).

However, Pablo takes a different view, "Without a body there would be no shame, suffering or death" (*Calderón* 96). For him, the existence of the body is proof of man's failure to be fully spirit, its mortality is proof of his fall, its gender is proof of its lack of wholeness. Without her body Rosaura could not be imprisoned, neither in the mental institution in the first and third sequences, nor in her shack in the second sequence, nor even in the bourgeois world of the play itself. Furthermore, man's animal nature only results in the birth trauma which typifies and symbolizes man's sense of alienation in life. Groppali notes that "coitus, podromo of birth, cannot help but reveal itself as evil" (*L'ossessione* 101).

Although sexual love may fail, Platonic love does have some redemptive power in *Calderón*, particularly as it is embodied in the character of Manuel, who is in love with Rosaura/Maria Rosa in the first and third sequences. Basilio claims Manuel wants "to finger her ass," but Manuel's love for her is idealistic, not animalistic. He does not want to impose on Rosaura what Groppali calls "the authoritarian . . . power of semen" (*L'ossessione* 101). To do so would only entrap her in another role, victimizing her further. Instead, Manuel liberates Rosaura from the enclosed world of the mental hospital twice. Rosaura claims, "I have been freed by a miracle / from the place where I was closed up" (*Calderón* 61). Manuel's love constitutes this miracle in its ability to create an opening in her universe. This love puts the closure of the bourgeois universe in perspective, refusing to accept its all-absorbing nature. He tells Basilio, "Please sir, don't confuse your bourgeois condition / with reality. It's an offensive identification" (*Calderón* 151).

However, any sense of Romantic-Platonic love far from dominates the play. Manuel is only a secondary character and he cannot accompany Rosaura into the ostensibly "real" world of her fourth reawakening. In this "real" world she realizes that she is not a daughter, or prostitute, or wife, or mother. Instead, her role in life is that of a victim. As such, she finds herself incarcerated in a Nazi prison camp. She describes her surroundings in a disturbingly graphic detail reminiscent of *Salò* or the more gruesomely atavistic scenes of *The Canterbury Tales*. She then recounts to Basilio her dream of the workers who, waving red banners and bearing food and clothes, come to free her and her fellow inmates. However, Pasolini does not conclude his play with this hope of revolution, but rather with the despair of closure. Basilio's final remarks verbalize the same sense of closure which the hermetic structure of the play itself has already demonstrated. He responds to Rosaura:

> All the other dreams you have dreamed or ever will dream
> could actually be real.
> But as for this dream of the workers, there can be no doubt:
> it is a dream, nothing but a dream.

> (*Calderón* 183)

5

Affabulation

First published in the periodical *Nuovi Argomenti* in 1967, *Affabulation* was not published in book form until 1977, together in a volume with *Pylades*. The play has been Pasolini's most successful with both critics and audiences. Pasolini himself was aware of the potential success of the play. Manacorda recounts, "Pasolini . . . says *Affabulation* seems to him the only one of his theatrical pieces that can still communicate to a vast, even general public" (81). The play has done just that, particularly in the two productions mounted by Vittorio Gassman. In fact, the popularity of *Affabulation* recalls Pasolini the fashionable filmmaker of the 1960s, the provocateur in an age of provocation. All the plays were conceived during this period, in conjunction with *Teorema*, but it is *Affabulation* which is most closely related to this quintessentially popular Pasolini film. Rinaldi writes, "*Affabulation* would thus seem identical to *Teorema* . . . the bourgeoisie upset by Something of the divine" (290). As in *Teorema*, the divine intrudes into the bourgeois world of *Affabulation* in the form of a beautiful fair-haired male youth. In both the film and the play the bearer of the divine is also the bearer of an unsettling sexuality. However, whereas Pasolini observes the effects of this divine sexuality on the entire household in *Teorema*, in *Affabulation* he focuses solely upon the reaction of the father, the authoritarian Laius figure, as he is led to abandon his social role in favor of irrational behavior. Superficial similarities can also be found between the film and the play, as both take place in and around Milan, and both conclude in a train station.

Of course, the similarities between *Teorema* and *Affabulation* alone do not account for the success of the latter. Instead, the play has probably been popular because it is Pasolini's most readily comprehensible, the least "open" as to the significance of its dramatic action. Siciliano calls it "a text which attempts to recompose the primary tragedy" ("Gassman"). This recomposition is actually an inversion of the primary tragedy of the death of the king. If *Calderón* is a contamination of *Las Meniñas* and *Life Is a Dream*, then *Affabulation* is a contamination of Sophocles' *Oedipus the King*. Numerous references to the ancient Greek tragedy are made during the course of the action of Pasolini's play and the Shade of Sophocles even appears in it as a character. However, as a contamination of Sophocles' tragedy, *Affabulation* is quite distinct from Pasolini's own cinematic version of *Oedipus the King*.

A recomposition of the primary tragedy, the plot of *Affabulation* is relatively simple, especially when compared to that of *Calderón*. In its own way, *Affabulation* is a virtual embodiment of Aristotle's dictum that tragedy be the imitation of a single and complete action, in this case the death of the prince. The play recounts the Father's obsession with his son. As his obsession progresses, he neglects his social obligations and even his social role. He attempts to provoke his son into killing him as a means of relieving himself of the obsession. When this fails, he then kills his son. Although this resolves the dramatic action, it does not solve his problems any more than Oedipus' discovery of who is responsible for the plague on Thebes solves his problems. Both protagonists are left at the end of their respective plays to confront themselves.

In the modern bourgeois universe of Pasolini's play the original Dionysian rite of kings is perverted into the death of the prince, as the role of king and prince are reversed. The Father in *Affabulation* claims:

> There are epochs in the world
> in which fathers degenerate
> *and if they kill their sons*
> *they commit regicide.*
>
> (*Affabulation* 106)

Affabulation is the only play in which Pasolini sets out specifically to observe the evolution of the death of the prince. The death of the prince is implicit in *Calderón*, *Pigsty* and even in *Pylades*, as these plays presuppose a closed universe and the death of the prince is assumed as a given. However, in *Affabulation* there is no character who presupposes such a closure, and so the play allows for at least the illusion of Aristotelian action.

Herein lies the difference between the arguably classical fate of *Affabulation* and the mannerist closure of the other plays. Although fate and closure are similar in their function of dictating the inevitability of events, they are different in viewpoint. Classical fate predicts these events from a viewpoint anterior to the action, while mannerist closure assumes, regardless of chronology, that the events have already occurred and are always occurring. Stella tells Rosaura with absolute certainty at the very outset of *Calderón* that no one will come to liberate her, that her identity, her entire world is a foregone conclusion, and, despite Manuel's love, Pasolini never seriously denies this assertion. In contrast, Oedipus is left to believe that he functions in an open universe and that he can act out of free will. Similarly, the Father has no idea at the beginning of *Affabulation* that he will kill his son. It is only in retrospect that Oedipus and the Father can perceive the inevitability of their fates.

Pasolini actually vacillates between a sense of mannerist closure and classic fatality in the play. He writes, "In my work there is an invariable and a variable. . . . The first corresponds to a type of fatality . . . the second corresponds to the disordered attempts to revolt against that fatality: be these hypocritical, insincere, naive, desperate or otherwise" (qtd. in Vallora 126–27). He toys with the concept of fate in the scene in the play where the Father, anxious for information about his son, goes to Pasolini's satiric version of the oracle at Delphi, a Fortune-teller:

FATHER: Your crystal ball couldn't be mistaken?
FORTUNE-TELLER: Sure it could, just like any crystal ball.

(Affabulation 88)

In a world which is believed to be open, fate becomes so arbitrary that it begins to resemble chance. The bourgeoisie rejects such seeming haphazardness, replacing the oracle with the computer, relying on reason rather than on intuition or inspiration to discern the inevitability of events. Therefore, as a bourgeois document the play is marked by a sense of deterministic closure, despite Pasolini's interest in exploring fate. Tian claims the action of the play is "little more than the symbolic gesture of a ritual predisposed beforehand" ("Conversazione"). Of course, this observation is just as valid for Sophocles' *Oedipus the King.* However, while the sequence of events in *Oedipus the King* is linear, *Affabulation* concludes with a sense of retrospection which reveals the events to be cyclical. The Father comments, "Let me / start all over again from the beginning" (*Affabulation* 114).

As the bourgeois reality of the Father exists in a fallen state and is already expressive of itself, the play as such becomes expressively redundant and pointedly metatheatrical. It self-consciously must represent itself with itself, as well as any dramatic action to which it may refer. The following Pirandellian interchange illustrates this:

> FATHER: Therefore, if I were to see my son as if . . .
>   on stage . . .
> SOPHOCLES: Your son *is already* on stage,
>   don't you realize? On a living stage. . . .
>   *He represents himself to you.*

(Affabulation 74–75)

The play is also kept in its metatheatrical perspective by curious passages of dialogue which are simultaneously within and outside the context of the represented reality of the dramatic action. The Mother refers to the Father's penchant for monologues and Sophocles claims he does not speak to the Father but to the Father's character. Furthermore, as a self-conscious bourgeois document, *Affabulation*, like *Calderón*, begins with a direct address to the audience. Like the Speaker, the Shade of Sophocles discusses aesthetic matters and makes apologies for the author. Like Basilio, the Father also addresses the audience directly about matters of philosophical, political or thematic relevance to the action of the play.

Irony inserts itself into this self-conscious and critical distance, undermining the sense of the tragic, reducing it with objectification and reason. Sophocles blames the fall of tragedy on the bourgeois literary tradition. He tells the Father:

> Excuse me if my wisdom is a bit ironic;
> but it is you who wants me so,
> corrupted by many centuries of irony, corrupted
> by Cervantes, by Ariosto, by Manzoni, heroes
> who are cautious and reduce everything
> because reason does not want to recognize mystery!

(Affabulation 71–72)

The Father begins as such a hero, cautious and wanting to reduce everything, but he cannot reduce the mystery of his son. He is an avid reader of the bourgeois literary tradition, especially partial to the sense of removal in Proust. The Father's irony is a symptom of his self-alienation, but it also serves him as a defense. His detachment ensures his survival and his success in a world which is itself detached. He prays:

> Our Father in Heaven,
> I've never been ridiculous in my life,
> I've always had a veil of irony over my eyes.

(Affabulation 38)

The Father fears the ridiculous. Two generations before Pasolini, the concept of "the fear of the ridiculous" was used by Chiarelli, Pirandello and the playwright Rosso di San Secondo to indicate that a character avoided being fully immersed in his social role so that he could discard it when it placed him in a dangerously ridiculous or ludicrous position. Despite the Father's consciousness of his role, his irony disintegrates and he acts in earnest. He loses his self-composure and makes a scene in a very un-Italian manner, "without even a little bit of playfulness," as the Mother points out (*Affabulation* 36). As the Father's playfulness and sense of irony desert him in enacting his role, he becomes ridiculous and evolves into a tragic hero. He explains:

> There is always, in the hero of a tragedy,
> a moment in which he is a little ridiculous,
> for which he is to be pitied.
>
> (*Affabulation* 107)

The audience is provoked to pity because it feels itself in some way superior to the tragic hero (e.g., the audience knows Oedipus' true identity before he does). However, this same feeling of superiority also risks making the tragic hero appear ridiculous.

The same sense of self-alienation which results in irony also results in silence. Existing in a fallen, nonprimal state, the bourgeoisie is already so self-expressive that verbal expression becomes redundant and unnecessary. The Father comments, "My behavior was detached from things and *I knew how to be silent.* / To defend myself, after irony, I had silence" (*Affabulation* 39). The pervasive silence of *Teorema* comes to mind. The Son describes the world of his bourgeois neighbors as one "of silent houses" hermetically enclosed in itself.

However, this sense of hermetic closure and self-containment is disrupted in *Affabulation*, as it is in *Calderón*, when the protagonist awakens from a dream with a scream. The result is again a birth trauma of existential proportions. The Father observes:

> Everything begins now with this dream. . . .
> A man born anew in that dream?
>
> I am no longer only myself. What has been added to me?
> Something I was before or should have been already?
>
> (*Affabulation* 12–13)

The dream leaves the Father with the realization that his "I is an other," jolting him out of the equilibrium of his irony, and freeing him from his bourgeois paralysis so that he can take action as Basilio could not. The dream is a product of what he was before, or should have been already, his pre-fallen self in which he was at one with himself and the world. As such, the dream cannot be reduced in the conscious state by his bourgeois use of reason. Indeed, the content of the dream remains a mystery to the audience and to the Father himself.

Nevertheless, he stipulates that he dreamed God. Believing God to be the content of his dream, he undergoes a sort of religious conversion, stripping himself, locking himself in his room for hours at a time and talking to Him. Such sincerely felt religious fanaticism disturbs his wife, who considers him mentally ill, much like Basilio thought Maria Rosa to be. It is not that the Mother is not religious, but her belief system is kept in check by bourgeois reason and is motivated not so much by spiritual need as by the social need to play the role of a believer in the community. She views her husband's behavior as a betrayal both of his social role and of the institutional and hierarchical religion of the church. She even calls for a priest to visit and cure him, but to no avail. The Father remains firm:

> As a savage interrogates the fire,
> or a peasant the sky, or a scientist
> the workings of his science:
> all those things in which the interest is pure.

> (*Affabulation* 92)

The interest of the savage, the peasant and the scientist is untainted by the ulterior utilitarian motives of the bourgeoisie. They make their interrogations because the process itself engages them and not because they wish to somehow exploit their findings. However, the Father's interest is not quite as pure as he would like to believe. Unlike Rosaura, the Father neither desires to retreat into his dreams nor insists that his real life transpires within his dreams. He does not content himself with the engagement his dreams offer him while unconscious. Instead, he attempts to recuperate his pre-fallen state in his waking existence, to make the dream rational, to know it cerebrally, empirically. A wealthy industrialist and capitalist, he views the dream as a commodity. In response, Sophocles chastises him for his "old damned habit of possession" (*Affabulation* 75). If the dream contains God, then God remains hidden in his dream and the Father cannot extract Him into his conscious bourgeois existence. God will not accompany him in his fall. No matter how much the Father talks to God, only the Shade of Sophocles will respond.

Ultimately, the Father believes his son is the key to unlocking the mystery of his dream. He comments, "I understand that it is in my son / that my dream continues" (*Affabulation* 18). The Father becomes as obsessed with his son as with the dream itself, seeking in his relationship with his son the same sense of primal integration he had experienced during his dream. He narcissistically wants his son to be like him, but the Son refuses. In fact, the Son does not even resemble his father physically. His blond hair, completely unlike the Father's, serves only as a haunting reminder to the Father of his own sense of isolation and alienation. Confronted with his separateness from his son, the astutely permissive Laius figure of the Father first attempts to absorb rather than challenge his Oedipal rival. He tries to engage his son by befriending him. The Son wisely resists this tactic. He tells his father, "I don't want your understanding! It's much / more dangerous, one knows, than your lack of understanding" (*Affabulation* 19).

Unable to establish any sort of love relationship between them such as that to which Rosaura had aspired, the Father hopes to establish a power relationship between himself and his son. He wants to dominate him, but Sophocles warns him:

> Of what use was it that my Oedipus
> solved the riddle? To take power?
> He took it and lost it.
>
> (*Affabulation* 70)

As with the dream, the Father views his son as an enigma to be solved, and thereby dissolved. However, Pasolini views man as an extra-empirical entity. He is composed of something which the bourgeoisie and its world cannot absorb. He is a mystery which, by its very nature, resists resolution. Sophocles admonishes the Father:

> Reason
> helps, in fact, in resolving enigmas.
> But your son—this is the point, I repeat—
> is not an enigma.
> *He is a mystery.*
>
> (*Affabulation* 69)

Departing from the bourgeois conception of a fallen and disintegrated universe, the Father cannot help persisting in his view of his son as something solely quantitative and not qualitative in nature, as an object.

Such, indeed, was his ironic and alienated view of himself prior to his dream.

However, the Son is not merely an object but a subject in his own right, and, as such, he remains as elusive to the Father as God Himself, defying reduction. The Son considers himself to be his own prime cause, holding himself aloof from his parents. The Mother claims he is "always ready to cut the cord" (*Affabulation* 16). Pasolini presents such behavior as no mere teenage rebellion. Instead, the Son's assertion of his independence has existential and even religious implications. The Son has never succumbed to the fall, but remains an entity of prime matter, a fully integrated individual who does not suffer from the divided nature of modern man. Like an animal, the Son is at one with the universe, completely instinctual, not suffering from the self-consciousness of the bourgeoisie to which he belongs. Like God, he looks to no authority higher than himself; he is omniscient. He and his girlfriend discuss him:

> SON: I was one of those children who,
>   and nobody knows how,
>   knows everything as soon as they are born. . . .
> GIRL: Then you don't think?
> SON: Right! But not because I don't want to know,
>   but because I do know.
>
> (*Affabulation* 100)

In his omniscience, he is immune to the bourgeois dependence on reason. Instead, he is a transcendent being, representing to the Father the transcendence and sense of integration he himself seeks.

Pasolini is careful not to neglect the animal component of man's nature in his search for integration and transcendence. The Son's spiritual potency, or even omnipotence, is not without its sexual counterpart. The Fortune-teller describes the Son as an untamed subproletariat type. She notes, "They have sex in the eyes, and the smell of semen /is in their uncombed, dusty hair" (*Affabulation* 79). The blondness of the Son's hair becomes an integral leitmotif in the play and several passages are devoted to it as an expression of both the Son's sexual prowess and his divinity. The Father notes:

> This terrible blond, not mine.
> It's here present, I could touch it,
> but it belongs to a different element
> like a bird in a cage, which belongs in Heaven.
>
> (*Affabulation* 17)

Pasolini's imagery again becomes Freudian, as flight serves him both as a metaphor for spiritual transcendence and the ability to maintain orgasm.

In contrast to the Son who is prodigious at flight in the conscious waking stage, so much so that he is "a bird," the Father must retreat into dreams in order to give free enough rein to his unsocialized libido in order to fly. He recounts a dream:

> I'm flying!
> I'm as light as a hollow, dried reed, I fly!
> I have no more bones—or else they're empty.
>
> (*Affabulation* 11)

However, outside the dream state, the Father is rendered impotent by the superior sexual capability of the Son. The Father concedes:

> If it weren't for his ever obscure youth
> . . . his unconfessed
> desire to fuck—that makes the boy,
> so young, more of a man than the man.
>
> (*Affabulation* 56)

Herein lies the reversal of the ancient Greek rite of kings in the play. The Father perceives his son to be the power figure who must be replaced, and himself as the oppressed. If he cannot dominate his son, then he will be dominated by him, as his bourgeois identity dictates that there must be some sort of hierarchical relationship between them. He gives his son a blatantly phallic knife, and then attempts to provoke the Son into using it against him.

However, the Son avoids taking any part in the Oedipus-Laius polemic. The Father realizes:

> Well, rather than wanting to kill my son . . .
> I wanted to be killed by him!! . . .
> And he, rather than wanting to kill me . . .
> neither wanted to kill me nor be killed by me.
>
> (*Affabulation* 111)

The Son refuses to play the Oedipus role, as he instinctively knows it would eventually embroil him into becoming a Laius figure, in making him equal to his father as his father wants. Instead of preaching revolution, the Son volunteers to do his military service, something which his father's influence and importance in the community could have spared him. He retains a sublime indifference to his father's power, neither challenging it nor championing it. Like Rosaura, he obeys without being obedient and disobeys without being disobedient. Only once does he lose his aloofness from his social role and allow his father to determine his behavior, by reacting against him and running away. As the Son's transcendent nature fails him, the Father wins a temporary victory. When the police escort the Son home, the Father tells him:

> Your body is heavy.
> You don't fly with the lightness of mysterious sons.
> You repeat me heavily in the world.
>
> (*Affabulation* 59)

Generally, however, the Father fails to engage his son. The Son's indifference to the Oedipus-Laius polemic leaves the Father alone to embody the intestinal struggle of the bourgeoisie within himself, as do the protagonists in *Orgy* and *Beast of Style*. Tian claims that "The Father . . . ends by assuming inside himself the entire dialectic of the drama" ("Conversazione"). The man-versus-man conflict in *Affabulation* evolves into a conflict of man versus himself.

Pasolini uses the Father, as the embodiment of the Oedipus-Laius polemic, to speculate on the Laius figure as a former Oedipus. The Father visits the Fortune-teller:

> FATHER: Why, don't you think Freud and Jung
> also studied fathers?
> FORTUNE-TELLER: Yes, but when these fathers were sons.
> . . . Little is known about the relationships of these fathers
> with those who are their *real fathers*, that is,
> excuse the banality, their male sons.
> There has always been a veil over this.
>
> (*Affabulation* 82–83)

Affabulation is Pasolini's attempt to remove this veil. The Father transfers his own Oedipal feelings once directed against his own father (i.e., the present Oedipus' grandfather) to the Son. Consequently, Pasolini reveals paternalism to be more exploitative than protective, as the Laius figure exorcises his once defeated, frustrated and repressed Oedipal feelings upon his own son.

Despite the empathy with which Pasolini treats his protagonist the Father, he retains his unqualified identification with the Son. Before Oedipus ever killed his father, he was abandoned by him and left to die in the wilderness with his feet bound. The Father is to blame for the

Oedipus-Laius conflict. Pasolini makes this explicit as he extrapolates the social and political significance of the action of his play in the Father's long concluding monologue:

> The great parliamentary democracies are armed to the teeth. . . .
> The fresh, humble, thirsty member
> is a scandal in itself when compared
> with that, old and flaccid, of its father.
>
> Thousands of sons are killed by their fathers: while
> every once in a while, a father is killed by his son—and this is what's noted.
> But how do fathers assassinate
> their sons? By means of prisons, trenches,
> concentration camps and bombed cities.
> And how do sons assassinate
> their fathers? By means of the innocent growth of their bodies
> which, newly arrived in the city, basically
> ask for nothing more than to be admitted.
> The son is thrown into the struggle against the father
> —and it's always the father who starts.
>
> (*Affabulation* 104)

Like *Calderón*, *Affabulation* may be indebted to Freud and Jung, but Pasolini is again careful not to discard Marx in the process. For him, the individual human psychology of the Oedipus-Laius polemic always has social and political figure implications. From birth trauma, the Oedipus figure is thrust into the pre-established discourse of "the struggle against the father." In bourgeois society, the Laius figures refuse to abdicate their social power to the more natural power of the young Oedipus figures, and the Oedipus figures are denied a franchise in power until they evolve into Laius figures. Whereas the Oedipus figures demand only the freedom to exist, the Laius figures have an agenda to control this existence, to reduce it or, if necessary, to eliminate it. Accordingly, the Father's monologue ends in a vision of an apocalypse.

Eventually the Father's attempts at assigning his son a role in this Oedipus-Laius conflict become overtly sexual. Pasolini goes beyond the incest of *Calderón* to toy with homosexual incest. At one point the Father confesses his homosexual attraction to his son, "I don't know you from the belt down" (*Affabulation* 60). For the Father, the Son's phallus becomes the Lacanian phallus, the "signifier of signifiers" that can render his dilemma comprehensible. As such, the Father refers to it as "the little sphinx in that glorious lap" (*Affabulation* 108). The Father thus displays strong jealousy toward his son's girlfriend and claims he feels cuckolded by their sexual activity. In fact, Pasolini focuses on the Oedipus-Laius bond to such an extent that the Jocasta role pales into relative insignificance. Although the Father flirts with his son's girlfriend, she astutely realizes that she is only a means for him to get to his son. She asks:

> But is this your real relationship?
> Because if so, it has to do with a love between the two of you:
> and I certainly have nothing to do with it.
>
> (*Affabulation* 30)

In the same vein, the Father refers to the Mother as "nothing but the bait above the trap" (*Affabulation* 54). In fact, he uses his wife in an elaborate scheme wherein he arranges for his son to view the two of them having intercourse.

When this plot fails and the Father cannot demonstrate his sexual potency to his son, he demands a demonstration of his son's sexual power. He convinces his son's girlfriend to allow him to watch as they make love. However, viewing the scene traumatizes the Father as it provides him with objective proof that his son is fully his own subject and not merely a narcissistic extension of the Father. Echoing the ideas of Lacan, Rinaldi comments, "The revelation of the phallus is therefore the apparition of the difference, engraving horror into a reality which is irreducible" (291). Reflected in the absoluteness of the Father's alienation from his son is the "irreducible reality" of his own fall, his alienation from himself. The Father attempts to negate his self-alienation by negating its reflection. In a manner reminiscent of Genet, if intimacy and immersion of self with self cannot be achieved with sex, then it can be achieved by murder. In his desperation to engage his son, he kills him with the knife, the only real transference of libido between them, but in the aftermath the Father's self-alienation still remains. Killing the Son cannot resolve the Oedipus-Laius conflict, for the Father carries it within him.

6

Pylades

The first of Pasolini's plays to be made available to the reading public, *Pylades* first appeared in the periodical *Nuovi Argomenti* in 1967. The play contains some beautiful lyric passages, but in some ways *Pylades* is the least poetic of Pasolini's dramas. In it Pasolini uses words more denotatively than connotatively, as he is primarily concerned with constructing arguments. The characters themselves are ciphers, representative of these arguments. Accordingly, the critic Paolo Emilio Poesio faults the play for being "too emblematic." This emblematic quality derives from the fact that it is essentially an allegory, as Pasolini examines the evolution of contemporary Italian society by creating a contamination of Aeschylus' *Oresteia*.

The play begins with the fall of fascism, as Argos, representing post–World War II Italy, awaits a new government. Aegisthus and Clytemnestra have been killed, even as Mussolini was assassinated and the Italian monarchy dissolved. Orestes arrives to bring a new order "from a nation more advanced / than mine, so backward and obsessed / with poverty and religion" (*Pylades* 149). The "nation more advanced" is a reference to the United States, and, accordingly, Orestes offers Argos democracy. He asserts, "The new revolution is not the work / of a few men, or a part of them / but of the entire city" (*Pylades* 208–9). Similarly, the entire population of Italy as a whole voted for a republic and a constitution.

This triumph of democracy inaugurates an age of positivism and Argos begins to thrive materialistically, creating an economy based on capitalism. Orestes' new order ushers in a boom not unlike the one experienced by postwar Italy during the 1950s:

> The work has provided unforeseen fruits.
> Palaces, factories, bridges shine with the whiteness

of materials never seen before. New technologies
are born.
The lifestyle changes every day.

(*Pylades* 225)

The success of postwar capitalism in Italy was made possible in part by
the defection of the Italian Socialist Party (PSI) from the political left to
take part in the coalition government with the more right-wing Christian Democrats who were supported by the Americans. Accordingly,
Pasolini refers to "Orestes, the socialist prince" ("Ceneri" 22).

By siding with the Christian Democrats, the PSI effectively excluded the communists, Italy's second-largest party, from government,
so that the government did not so much represent the masses of the
people as it fostered the power structure of bourgeois capitalism. As
such, it did not create what the PCI would consider a truly egalitarian
system. Similarly, although Orestes claims to bring a new order, he
retains as much power in the new democratic Argos as he would have
had in the old regime. The name and ideology of the power structure
may have changed, but the power structure remains as hierarchical as
that of the old monarchical order. Rinaldi notes, "The boom of the
post-war period triumphs until one realizes that this happy progress is
just the same old injustice of Agamemmnon, Aegisthus and Clytemnestra (fascism)" (294).

Pasolini blames the failure to create a truly egalitarian system on
the populace itself, whose passive complicity supports the new hierarchy. The chorus recriminates itself, "But are . . . we any better? / If we
don't do anything else / but wait for a new authority" (*Pylades* 118).
Pylades argues that the masses voted for democracy only because the
authoritarian figure of Orestes told them to do so. The two confront one
another:

ORESTES: But these are the people who elected us!
PYLADES: Who advised them in voting?
        Who was beside them? Athena perhaps?
        No, still beside them, as always,
        was a tangle of vipers.

(*Pylades* 151)

The bourgeoisie subtly purports to represent the masses in order to
maintain its own power and authority.

The new and affluent materialistic society which Orestes encourages in Argos is based on reason. He advocates the rejection of the old
gods in favor of Athena. Born full-grown from the head of Zeus, Athena

is not the product of animal passion, but of pure cerebral rationalism. She is the goddess of reason and, as such, ushers in an enlightened age. Orestes praises her:

> She is not lost in the darkness of centuries.
> She has come to light. . . .
> Her hour . . .
> is the heart of the day, and her cult
> does not require sanctuaries isolated in the fields:
> instead her temples are the markets, squares,
> banks, schools, stadiums, ports
> and factories.
>
> (*Pylades* 121–22)

Religion is, in effect, secularized in a society which has disengaged its political power structure from spiritual precepts. Argos represents all democracies which have abandoned divine right and the Great Chain of Being in favor of a separation of church and state. Electra is forced to concede, "The Furies in the temple, Athena in the parliament" (*Pylades* 186).

This separation is tantamount to the fall itself; it is a symptom of the disintegrated universe. Orestes' promotion of reason insinuates itself into the existential void which is perceived as resulting from this disintegration. Insofar as Argos and, by extension, all laissez-faire democracies are based on reason, they reflect this existential void. The chorus asks Orestes:

> But what did the populace of Athens say
> finding itself no longer with a king in power
> who based his authority on the terror of the old gods?
> What did the populace say, seeing itself abandoned to itself?
>
> (*Pylades* 127)

In both the existential void and democracy, man must take final and ultimate responsibility for his actions, as his world is not part of a larger whole but is, instead, his own arbitrary and hermetic creation.

Consequently, justice is no longer divine; it is reasonable. Orestes can therefore be acquitted of the murders of Aegisthus and Clytemnestra by a human jury, as the jurors cannot call upon a god for their verdict but are abandoned to themselves to determine guilt or innocence. In *The Flies*, the French philosopher and dramatist Jean-Paul Sartre asserted that man carries his own punishment with him. In *Pylades*, Pasolini presents the logical corollary of Sartre's assertion, that if man can condemn himself, he can also absolve himself. The chorus in *Pylades* tells

Orestes that "you are the inventor of your freedom" (181).

However, inasmuch as Orestes' innocence is reasonable it is also arbitrary, as any application of reason in a universal void is arbitrary. Athena herself challenges Orestes' faith in reason by taunting him with its arbitrariness, hermeticism and profound disengagement. She instructs him, "Reason, you know, loves to play with words / as it cannot play with things" (*Pylades* 187). In another passage she tells him, "Not only / does it play with words, but it also plays with the reasoning process itself!" (*Pylades* 192). In fact, Athena delights in wordplay and in pursuing arguments which are ambiguous, equivocal and even absurd, but nevertheless logical.

Despite Orestes' acquittal, a concept of original sin persists in the play. Pylades warns Orestes:

> *Your spirit turns back. . . .*
> You don't see the Furies
> because they are too close to you. . . .
> And if Athena has enlightened you with her pure Reason,
> you remain impure
> because your past continues in you.
>
> (*Pylades* 152–53)

Orestes' legal innocence does not bring him spiritual innocence. His reliance on reasonable processes cannot purge his soul, nor does his championing of Athena mean that the Furies no longer exist. In fact, the triumph of reason is placed in doubt when the Furies return to plague the countryside.

Confronted with the persistence of the Furies in his new rational world, Orestes attempts to pacify them by sublimating them and repressing them in the dream state, where the irrational and primal impulses that the Furies represent can be given free rein. Sleep thus becomes a form of worship to the Furies. Orestes claims, "*In no other way do we love more purely than in sleep*" (*Pylades* 124). Dreams are again, as in *Calderón,* the place where the original self still exists and can be at one with its world. However, by relegating the irrational to the unconscious, Orestes renders it ineffectual in the external, waking world. In this way the Furies can no longer pose a threat to the rational materialism of the new Argos. Orestes is thus astutely permissive, as dreams become the bourgeois means of absorbing the irrational.

Electra is the champion of the old order. Pasolini describes "the regression of Electra / the daughter who loved her father-king and is now a fascist" ("Ceneri" 22). Unlike Orestes, she embraces her share of the guilt for the murders of Aegisthus and Clytemnestra. Prior to

Orestes' arrival, her life consisted of daily pilgrimages between her parents' graves and the church. She has even reversed herself, honoring her mother for having played her part in the rite of kings. She says, "But now that she is dead, she is queen again" (*Pylades* 130). The rite has served to reintegrate Clytmnestra with the universe. Groppali notes that "to kill means to conform to the harmony of the cosmos" (*L'osses-sione* 67). Death offers transcendence. It purges man of his imperfection and his fall. With her passionate and instinctual reverence for the dead, Electra seems to embody Lacan's dictums that "death constitutes in the subject the eternalization of his desire," and that in it one's life "takes on all the meaning it has" (104, 105). In accord with this philosophy, Electra and her followers dress in black. She cherishes spiritual and irrational ritual, and even the ancient curse on her house. This curse offers her a sense of harmony with the pre-fallen universe. For her, it is a manifestation of some larger master plan. She believes that when Orestes abdicates his role in the rite of kings and its accompanying guilt, he must also give up any sense of a pre-fallen universal harmony and the integration it ostensibly could offer him.

Despite Electra's reactionary, even fascistic position, Pasolini does not treat her with antipathy, but instead appreciates her for her belief in the spiritual and in an original, integrated universe. Pasolini claims "a bad religion is still a religion" ("The Enigma of Pius XII," *Le poesie* 67). Here Pasolini openly attacks Marx's famous dictum that "religion is the opiate of the people," accusing classical communist ideology of promoting the same reductive materialism championed by bourgeois capitalism. Both are the products of reason and presuppose an insuper-able universal fall. Instead, Electra advocates a religion that is nonutili-tarian, primordial and natural. It rejects the cerebral self-consciousness of Orestes' bourgeois society, even as it rejects reason. Groppali aptly compares Electra to Pasolini's Medea, claiming that both aim at "com-municating with an abstract universe by means of signs and symbols" (*L'ossessione* 78).

Electra's religion is inspired by the light of dawn and dusk, leaving the cult of Athena the light of the "heart of day." Whereas Athena's daylight provides enlightenment, the inspiration offered by the bril-liance of the sun on the horizon is blinding in its intensity. Orestes notes of Electra's followers that "the same source of light which blinds them is exalted / as rigid as certain insane priests, but nonetheless purified /by their own irrational and fanatic hate" (*Pylades* 135). The moderation of Orestes' reason is countered by the potentially destructive excess of Electra's passion. His positivism polarizes her religion into an increas-ingly nihilistic position, which she nevertheless defends. She claims that "in my hate / there is more love than in all your fraternity" (*Pylades* 132). Her hate at least offers engagement and is eternal, whereas his fraternity offers only alienation and is ephemeral.

In a paradoxically positivistic manner, Orestes attempts to put her hate to use. He forms an alliance of convenience with her in order to take advantage of her soldiers. In accord with the fascist ideal, they are the fiercest, motivated not by capital gain, but by sentiments of atavistic patriotism. It is only by means of this alliance that Orestes is able to defeat Pylades' revolutionaries.

Although Orestes is young and interested in establishing a new order in Argos, it is Pylades who is the Oedipus figure in the play. As Orestes' new democratic society evolves, Pylades becomes the provocateur who seeks to represent those who are disenfranchised by the new system. Like Pasolini, Pylades speaks for the subproletariat, the lower classes and the peasantry of the countryside. However, also like the bourgeois-born Pasolini, Pylades is not really a member of those classes he claims to represent. A boyhood friend of the prince Orestes, Pylades was instead born into the upper classes. In fact, the chorus distrusts the political altruism of Pylades' motives for seeking to incite revolution. They warn Orestes:

> Or was it a desire for power which
> he could not realize in any other way? . . .
> He wants to be you.
>
> (*Pylades* 160)

Jealous of Orestes' power, the Oedipal Pylades is exposed as a would-be Laius. Athena even claims that Pylades is faithful to her in his own way.

Pylades sympathizes with those excluded from power because he himself suffers from a sort of exclusion which, however, is perhaps more existential than political in its origins. Pylades' superior intellect torments him with an acute awareness of his own sense of self-alienation and ironic bourgeois detachment. He declares, "I am a soul in pain / —and I'm not even sure / of the sincerity of my grief" (*Pylades* 170). Pylades responds to this sense of alienation by rejecting the rules of bourgeois social behavior that repress the animal-man and exploit the contradictions of the divided self. He refuses an identity which is contingent upon a social context and spurns the respectable society which is his birthright in favor of the more asocial, even underworld, elements of the new Argos. The chorus describes Pylades' behavior as being not unlike Pasolini's patronage of the subproletariat teenage boy prostitutes in Rome:

It seems that he, refusing our daughters in full flower,
has made love with girls as eager as gypsies,
with paid women—like horrible mothers—
in order to violate them and himself.

(*Pylades* 160)

Pylades turns to sex as something irrational and irreducible. Although his sexual behavior makes him a social pariah, he prefers this social alienation to the keen and constant sense of existential self-alienation that proper society inflicts upon him.

Pylades is too acutely aware that the triumph of reason is contingent upon the sacrifice of an integrated universe for him to content himself with it. He looks at the material progress of Argos and sees only its spiritual fall. For him, the power structure of Orestes' bourgeois democratic society is a fabrication, an artifice. In contrast to Orestes' positivistic approach, Pylades asserts:

I am nothing other than the servant of reality,
I follow it, watch it, I have no authority
to reduce it in my power and to know it!

(*Pylades* 155)

Pylades does not accept human justice. He rejects Orestes' authority to find himself innocent. He does not want to reduce reality so that he can master it with a system of rational processes. Instead, he is the servant of a reality beyond his control, subject to the unknown and unknowable forces behind it.

Like Electra, Pylades gravitates to a sort of nihilism when confronted with Orestes' new materialistic society. He claims that he has "a blind / irrational desire to destroy" (*Pylades* 156). Also like Electra, he realizes that death reintegrates man with the universe. He comments, "It is ONE—I know now— / the place where one is born and where one dies" (*Pylades* 231). He rejects, as does Electra, the light of the "heart of day" propagated by Orestes. Consequently, although Pylades is a radical and Electra is a reactionary, they eventually find a common ground in the very extremeness of their positions as they counter Orestes' moderation and reasonableness. Although Electra emphasizes the spiritual and Pylades emphasizes the animal, both attempt to resuscitate the irrational as a means of combatting Orestes' cerebrality. They unite because of their individual inability to overcome the fall and rob Orestes of his power. Separately, they may be impotent, but together they hope to complement one another. However, two parts fail to make a whole, as their union becomes merely a double expression of their combined impotence. Their political alliance results only in the failure of revolution.

Similarly, their sexual relationship results only in the failure of orgasmic transcendence. They are what Lacan has called "sexed partial beings." Santato observes, "Pylades and Electra are united by an analogous destiny of incompleteness: respectively, the frustrated male and the female succubus" (272). Far from being ethereal and Romantic, their sex deteriorates into a desperate sadomasochistic insistence on escaping the rational, a feigning of truer integration. Pylades notes:

> The violence of the flesh drags me
> with my semen, outside myself,
> in an escape which attempts to liberate me
> with something nauseating and impure.
>
> (*Pylades* 219)

Groppali describes a similar process at work in Electra, as he again compares her to Pasolini's Medea. Groppali claims that "the priestess degrades into a woman-animal, searching in sex for a burning substitute capable of engraving a sign in the universe" (*L'ossessione* 78). In contrast to his earlier masturbation and her celibacy, their sex is "nauseating and impure" because its procreative nature is an affirmation of their fall, imperfection and mortality. As such, their union is actually a form of resignation and self-negation. Heterosexuality is thus shown to provide a reintegration of the self with the universe which is as nihilistic as that offered by the rite of kings—death. Appropriately enough, Pylades and Electra are first united in a cemetery.

In contrast, the nonprocreative love between Pylades and Orestes is pure. They are the true complements of one another which, together, would create an integrated whole. Orestes is tall, blond, glorious and agile, while Pylades is sturdy, dark, brooding and ardent. As is typical in Pasolini, their complementary physical characteristics merely reflect their more profoundly complementary spiritual natures. Their sexual union would provide the spiritual transcendence Pylades futilely seeks with Electra. Groppali refers to "sexual inversion as the double possession of the phallus, the proud self-knowledge of absolute virility" (*L'ossessione* 74). The absoluteness of this virility implies the possibility of a recuperation of the fall.

However, Pylades and Orestes are never united, neither spiritually, nor politically, nor sexually, despite the profound bond between them going back to their childhood. At that age the adult self-consciousness of their social roles had not yet manifested itself. They were not aware of women as the other, but only of themselves and each other as secondary narcissistic extensions of themselves. Pasolini alludes to that period prior to their fall into adulthood "when women were unknown / and they abandoned themselves to discussions of love and the soul / which have nothing to do with the present reality" ("Ceneri" 22–23).

In one sense, as narcissistic extensions of each other, Pylades and Orestes are actually the same person. Their division into two characters represents the divided nature of man and his self-alienation. When Pylades leaves him, Orestes realizes, "The Furies have subtracted me from myself" (Pylades 164). Similarly, Pylades also suffers from a Lacanian sense of "I is an other" and he transitivistically yearns for that part of himself which is Orestes. An advocate of reason, Orestes weeps after his meetings with Pylades. A believer in the irrational, Pylades combats Orestes with logical argumentation. They are yin and yang, each tainted with the essence of the other, so that the roles they play in the Oedipus-Laius polemic are impure. As the Oedipus figure, Pylades is a potential Laius; as a Laius figure, Orestes is a former Oedipus. Oedipus and Laius are one and the same in their origins, and so are Pylades and Orestes. The Oedipus-Laius dialectic again remains unresolved.

However, Pasolini does resolve the action of his play when Pylades' revolution ends in defeat. Pylades aspires to an existential and political transcendence which Pasolini describes in the same Freudian flight imagery that he used in Calderón and Affabulation. Orestes calls Pylades an "eagle who now flies toward the void" (Pylades 210). When Orestes defeats him, he tells him:

> Naive Pylades! The feelings which drove you . . .
> are now gathered in you
> in their highest and most extreme maturity.
>
> It is precisely at this point that they lose their meaning.
>
> I am here to collect you, with these tremendous words,
> like a hunter who kills a bird
> exactly at the moment in which its flight is highest and most secure.
>
> (Pylades 206–7)

Transcendence is impossible and the closure established by Orestes remains firm. Defeated, Pylades himself begins to suspect that the fall is universal and not merely a product of bourgeois society. He asserts, "The world is guilty and the dawn is false" (Pylades 235).

It is this sense of deflation and disillusionment which marks the conclusion of Pasolini's play. Aware of his yin-yang connection to Orestes, and his need for a power structure against which he can rebel in order to play the Oedipus role, Pylades is paralyzed by the dubiousness of his own sincerity. He is as much defeated by his own bourgeois self-consciousness and objectivity as he is by Orestes. He observes:

> I should ask myself how,
> if this is a tragedy,
> it does not close with new blood.
>
> I should ask myself what sense
> there is in an intrigue of existence
> which searched so much for truth
> and now dissolves itself
> *in pure and simple uncertainty.*

(Pylades 234)

Neither he nor Orestes can shed one another's blood, as they need one another to pursue the Oedipus-Laius polemic, not to a climax, but as a continual intestinal struggle. As Canali would assert, the tragedy of the play thus lies in its inability to be tragic.

Pylades begins as Pasolini's most explicitly dialectical and diacritical play. Its structure is a virtual sequence of theses-antitheses-syntheses. However, Pasolini penetrates and dissolves this dialectic with a revelation not unlike that of Brecht in his conclusion of *The Good Woman of Setzuan*. Athena comments, "Between the love of liberty and the necessity of things / there is a thin line . . . / Or rather, you will do evil to achieve good" (*Pylades* 193). Conventional tragedy thus becomes obsolete as this all-encompassing, deflationary, bourgeois ethic replaces the dialectic of confrontation that has traditionally characterized Western drama.

7

Pigsty

Pigsty was not published until 1979, together in a volume with *Orgy* and *Beast of Style*. Nevertheless, in 1969 *Pigsty* became the first of Pasolini's dramatic texts to be seen by a vast audience, as he adapted the play for the cinema, using the same title. Although the film received a considerable degree of critical attention at the time, it has not proved to be as enduring as many of his other films. In fact, the film has deterred rather than encouraged production of the play, which has never been produced. *Pigsty* is arguably both Pasolini's worst film and his worst play. Of course, a cinematic adaptation need not necessarily be merely a filmed version of the play, but the film of *Pigsty* is virtually just that. Pasolini used the dramatic text verbatim in the film, diverging only in the substitution of the cannibal sequence on Mount Etna for the play's confrontational scene between the protagonist, Julian, and the philosopher Spinoza.

The plot of the play and the textual part of the film takes place in the 1960s, focusing upon Julian, the son of a wealthy German industrialist. He is courted by Ida. As Ida hails from an equally wealthy family, his parents deem her a suitable match for him. However, he remains obstinately aloof to her advances, preferring pigs as his sexual partners and making daily trips down to the pigsty. Klotz, his father, has recently discovered the true identity of his business rival, Herdhitze. Herdhitze is actually Hirt, a former Nazi death-camp officer. For his part, Herdhitze has discovered Julian's perverted sexual interest in pigs. Klotz and Herdhitze transform their potential mutual blackmail into a complicity of silence and a business partnership beneficial to both. In the meanwhile, Julian continues his excursions to the pigsty until he meets his death, gruesomely eaten by pigs.

However, the most effective parts of the film are the scenes of cannibalism not found in the play. Pasolini uses cannibalism hyperbolically as an extreme expression of the ethic of conflict traditionally used

in Western drama in general, the same ethic of conflict which he pene-
trated in *Pylades*. The nature of the conflict in *Pigsty* is made explicitly
Oedipal when one of the captured cannibals exclaims, "I have killed
my father, I have eaten human flesh, and I tremble with joy" (*Pigsty*,
Film dell'Orso). He exults in his Oedipal role, having successfully defied
absorption into the Laius-dominated bourgeois society below. The deso-
late and elemental landscape of Mount Etna not only provides the cannibal with a refuge from bourgeois society, but, as a volcanic generator
of prime matter, it also provides the filmmaker Pasolini with a visual
correlative for the primal behavior of his characters.

In order to avoid the fall into bourgeois self-consciousness, the
cannibals have attempted to transcend man's divided self by denying
their spiritual and intellectual natures, becoming completely animalistic.
Roncaglia notes that "to live without the word is a subhuman condition,
that of being a 'perfect animal'" (19). As perfect animals, the cannibals
eschew "the first social contract" of language. Having eaten the flesh
of the father, they have in essence ingested Lacan's "Law of the Father"
as well. As a result, the scenes on Mount Etna are totally without the
relatively unimportant code of verbal dialogue.

Barthes has asserted that "a code cannot be destroyed, only 'played
off'" (*Image* 144). In the text of his play, Pasolini uses language ab-
stractly, toying with it in a manner reminiscent of Ionesco, as existential
Angst gives way to giddiness. *Pigsty* does not begin, as do some of the
other plays, with a scream, but with a whistle, and Pasolini maintains
this rather ironic tone throughout most of the text. Rinaldi notes, "Here
the poetry does not even dare to take itself seriously, not even as a form
of consolation, but instead gently makes fun of itself, overdoing itself
in rhyme" (306). In fact, the play's dialogue periodically degenerates
into a series of inane rhymes and tra-la-las. Julian and Ida even play a
game of renaming one another, pointing up the arbitrary and provi-
sional nature of signification and identification. The playfulness of signification extends to identification as well. Lacan has argued that "the
imperative of the Word . . . has formed man in its image" (106). Being
contingent upon his name, man's identity becomes precarious. Accordingly, Klotz observes that Herdhitze's name means "oven heat" in German, a macabre reference to his former involvement with Nazi concentration camps. Another character is even named "Ding," meaning
"thing."

It is this degeneration of language which has prompted Rinaldi to
call the text of *Pigsty* "perfectly useless" (305). However, if the text is
useless, it is because the words which comprise it are themselves useless. In the process of purifying the word, Pasolini attempts to liberate

it of reference to anything other than itself. Words become themselves the signified, and as they do so, they cease to be signifiers. However, as words cease to signify anything other than themselves, they verge on obsolescence, no longer functioning and deteriorating into meaningless sound. The critic Jean-Michel Gardair comments that "the liberated word is the subversive word, subverting its own self" ("Il *Porcile*," in Luzi 391). Despite Barthes, Pasolini seems to observe that if language is "played off" too extensively, this "playing off" eventually results in an effective dismantling of the codal system code which makes language understandable in the first place. As sign-words are abused, they can signify anything, which means they actually signify nothing. Accordingly, both the play and the film end in a complicity of silence, with Herdhitze shushing the peasants who would otherwise recount the details of Julian's death.

Gardair claims that the degeneration of the dialogue in the play merely reflects the "social alienation of the word" (391). Indeed, words do encounter the impasse of social behavior and are molded by it. Klotz and Herdhitze remain ridiculously polite with one another under all circumstances. At one point Klotz even prevents Herdhitze from recounting the details of his own son's perversion. He comments, "Enough. We have reached the point where it seems / impossible for you to continue and for me to listen" (*Pigsty* 65). Furthermore, words are presented as dissociated from their primal meanings because man is dissociated from his primal self. Both deteriorate into form without content. Man's "name" and social role usurp his humanity, and the characters become virtual cartoons. Klotz describes himself and his wife as caricatures by George Grosz, the German New Realist artist of the 1920s. Klotz speaks with the cold objectivity that is symptomatic of his self-alienation:

> I might very well have been drawn by Grosz
> in the form of a huge pig, and you like a fat
> sow: at dinner, naturally, I with my
> secretary's ass on my knee, and you with
> the chauffeur's prick in your hand.

(*Pigsty* 24)

Grosz was a designer for Brecht, and Brecht is referred to several times in the play. In fact, the play is a contamination of Brecht's concept of the *Lehrstück*. The sense of dissociation which pervades Pasolini's use of language and characterization in the play is merely his own approximation of a Brechtian *Verfremdungseffekt*, as the audience is supposed to learn from the parable of the play without empathizing with the characters. The film version of *Pigsty* creates a dialectic between the lack of emotional empathy in the textual sequence and the extreme, rarefied empathy, played solely upon the senses, in the cannibal sequence. Gardair observes that "the *grand guignol* is the exact opposite of Brechtian dramaturgy" (390). However, both the *grand guignol* and Brecht's *Lehrstück* are rooted in the hyperbole of the grotesque. *Pigsty* is most appropriately read not, like the other plays, as an attempt at modern tragedy, but as a grotesque.

Pigsty is distinct from the other plays not only in Pasolini's treatment of the subject matter, but also because, while the protagonists of the other plays tragically and naively hope that an opening in the universal bourgeois closure is possible, Julian knows with certainty from the outset it is not. Despite his youth, he does not, like Pablo and Pylades, champion revolution. Instead, he refuses to play a role in the Oedipus-Laius polemic, keenly aware of its yin-yang nature. He declines Ida's insistent invitation to accompany her to the student demonstrations in Berlin:

> I don't have opinions.
> I tried to have some, but I was only
> doing my duty. So I realized that
> even as a revolutionary I was a conformist.
>
> (*Pigsty* 16)

Instead of conformism or anticonformist conformism, Julian aspires to a true nonconformism as a means of maintaining an aloofness that will render his Laius-figure father impotent to combat or absorb him. His father concedes, "With a son who neither consented nor dissented / I could do nothing" (*Pigsty* 40). In fact, Julian is so disengaged from his social role that even maintaining appearances does not threaten him, and his willingness to do so further prevents his father from taking a polemical stance against him.

However, unlike the Son in *Affabulation,* Julian is not naturally aloof to the Oedipus-Laius polemic. Instead, his indifference is deliberate, tactical, as he attempts to combat the closure of the bourgeois universe with his own personal closure, by refusing to respond in any way to his social environment. Herdhitze describes him as having "closed himself inside a long, hermetic adolescence" (*Pigsty* 63). Having witnessed the abuse of language in the social role-playing of the bourgeoisie, Julian realizes the futility of verbal expression. As a result, he enters into a nonresponsive silence and remains noncommunicative for a considerable part of the play. He says quite simply, "Talking about myself hurts me" (*Pigsty* 8). With his silence, Julian seems to come to the realization that consciousness, or at least self-consciousness, and subjectivity are mutually exclusive. He subscribes to Lacan's anti-Cartesian assertion that "I am where I do not think" (166). In order to exist more fully, Julian abandons thinking.

Julian embraces his resultant catatonia as a calculated and suitable response to the paralytic immobility of the bourgeoisie. He tells Spinoza, "I don't make any decisions" (*Pigsty* 86). Decision-making presupposes a freewill which Julian knows the all-absorbing power of the fallen bourgeois universe renders impossible. Like Basilio in *Calderón*, he knows that any ostensibly polemical position is insincere and ephemeral. Instead, he prefers the integrity of outward passivity. The process is essentially one of mental withdrawal, a withdrawal not totally unlike Rosaura's. Like Rosaura, Julian takes refuge in a peaceful psychosis that provides him with a sense of integration similar to that of the dream state. His father diagnoses his catatonia, "My son is sleepy, nothing else but very sleepy" (*Pigsty* 59). However, sleep itself does not make Julian feel at one with the world; instead, he has nightmares.

Consequently, Julian's primary means of resurrecting his primal self is not in dreams, but in sex. He refers to himself as a slave of his penis. Like the cannibals in the film version, he avoids the divided self by submerging himself completely within his animal nature. Sexuality allows him to transcend bourgeois self-consciousness, and Pasolini again describes this transcendence in terms of Freudian flight imagery. Julian refers to his "continual, infinite happiness. / . . . the flight of eagles" (*Pigsty* 71). However, this happiness is not, in fact, continual. Orgasm cannot be maintained and Julian interprets its aftermath in traumatic, even apocalyptic terms. The fall of the individual man from orgasmic transcendence is tantamount to the fall of the universe itself. He confesses to Spinoza:

> Oh, how much seed I must throw! How much flesh
> in the bottom of my groin must experience the spasm,
> the lurid mechanical miracle which for others
> has such a circumscribed value! . . .
> But after love, the various colors of the world
> are intolerable colors—the sky after the explosion
> of the atomic bomb.

> (*Pigsty* 75)

Julian does not purge himself of his bourgeois fall even in the exaltation of the primal animal side of his nature. His perverse predilection for pigs is presented as a manifestation of the bourgeois heritage by which he remains irrevocably tainted. Julian merely transforms the spiritual and existential perversion of his parents into a sexual perversion. In a macabre and ironic moment, Klotz and Herdhitze drink to the health of Jews and pigs, both of which have inadvertently contributed to their success in the bourgeois social order. Spinoza queries as to whether this order is not "the true pigsty." The subject of pigs, in fact, provides Pasolini with a running gag for his play. Klotz refers to the Germans as "great sausage consumers" and Herdhitze reports that "Minister Ribbentrop grunted." Finally, Klotz speaks of his "womb large enough to contain an entire social class" (*Pigsty* 57). The pig thus becomes Pasolini's metaphor for the all-absorbing power of the bourgeoisie.

The business partnership of Klotz and Herdhitze epitomizes the all-absorbing power of the bourgeoisie, as the order regenerates itself by transforming Nazism into the German Economic Miracle. Klotz was raised in the bourgeois humanistic tradition. He calls the city of Cologne an "Athens of cement" and Herdhitze describes the Klotz estate as "Goethian." Klotz is a shrewd businessman who has exploited laissez-faire philosophy as a means of maintaining his power despite the seemingly cataclysmic historical changes of his time. He praises his own adaptability:

> This isn't Hitler's Germany!
> Tenderness and hardness are mixed.
> We make wool, cheese, beer and buttons
> (and the manufacture of cannons is now an export industry).
>
> (*Pigsty* 25)

Pasolini implies that Nazism and capitalism are merely two different manifestations of the same phenomenon. Each is an artificial, hermetic and ultimately arbitrary power structure wherein the common man is delegated the role of object. In Nazism he is an *Opfer* ("sacrifice"), while in capitalism he is a worker-consumer.

In contrast to Klotz, Herdhitze is a technocrat who was not born into wealth or the bourgeois cultural heritage. He learned scientific efficiency while a death camp officer. Potentially he could be an Oedipus character, offering a new order to replace that of the Laius-figure Klotz. However, Herdhitze's ostensibly new order is actually only an extension of Klotz' old order, as both men quickly realize. Despite the apparent material advances of the workers, they remain as subservient as ever to those who truly have power. The technicians of a modern economy have merely taken the place of the peasants of the past. Klotz and Herdhitze toast the ability of the bourgeoisie to regenerate itself, rendering all challenges to its authority ephemeral:

> KLOTZ: To our youth, Mr. Herdhitze!
> HERDHITZE: To our NEW youth, Mr. Klotz.
>
> (*Pigsty* 53)

A true dialectic is possible only in the scene between Julian and Spinoza, as Spinoza visits Julian in much the same manner that Sophocles visits the Father in *Affabulation*, outside the realm of the represented bourgeois reality of the play. As words are no longer subjected to the bourgeois "social alienation of the word," they may again function as signifiers. Consequently, both Julian and Spinoza can construct arguments which are not merely a superfluous, masturbatory verbal exercise.

Quoting from his *Ethics*, Spinoza feebly attempts to reason with Julian. Spinoza ostensibly concedes, "*Nothing must remain but God, nothing else but God*" (*Pigsty* 89). Nevertheless, Spinoza departs from the rationalistic assumption that God is an enigma rather than a mystery, and he attempts to explain Him. In fact, he claims that explaining God is the "mission" of reason. However, if God is resolved, He is dissolved. To Julian, such a reducible concept of God seems virtually indistinct from the existential void. Eventually, Spinoza is even constrained to describing to Julian "the pure and solitary presence of a God who does not console" (*Pigsty* 89). Spinoza's arguments are self-defeating and even self-incriminating. As he champions the same use of reason which has encouraged bourgeois society to thrive, he must eventually accept responsibility for "the true pigsty" of the world created by Klotz and Herdhitze.

In contrast to Spinoza, Julian is interested in "a language which / no Reason can explain" (*Pigsty* 88). For him, this "language" is God Himself and the primal unity He represents. Spinoza cannot deter Julian from the religious martyrdom he seeks. Pasolini wrote, "I am a priest and a free man, two reasons not to live" ("La Dansa di Narcìs II," *Gioventù* 217). Julian follows a similar credo. He is aware from the premonition of his nightmarish dreams that his sexual encounters with pigs will eventually result in his death, yet he intentionally persists. Like masturbation and homosexuality, bestiality is a nonprocreative form of sex. It is a "pure" love which, however, provides Julian with only an intermittent and temporary sense of self-integration and transcendence. However, the obliviousness of the death to which these encounters will lead constitutes, for him, a transcendence which is permanent. As a form of transcendence and liberation, death is welcomed. Spinoza tells him, "Go ahead and die then, if you want to, leave the world / . . . in a masturbation / or a mystic rapture" (*Pigsty* 87).

Masturbation and mystic rapture, as the ecstatic assertion of the primal animal and spiritual self, attempt to overcome the fall. However, self-assertion and self-negation paradoxically present themselves as one and the same thing, as the transcendence provided by Julian's spiritualism and bestiality is contingent upon his self-sacrifice or suicide. Julian experiences the universe as "a defect in the purity of Non-Being" (Lacan 317). Consequently, he purports to find God by negating himself as an entity diacritically distinct from Him, but Pasolini is not so sure. For his part, Pasolini does not poeticize about pigs as he did about homosexuality in *Affabulation* and *Pylades*, or about dreams and love in *Calderón*. Instead, he emphasizes the dubiousness of the success of Julian's martyrdom-transcendence by undermining it with his ironically pervasive *Verfremdungseffekt*, turning it into a macabre joke. Although the prince again dies, this time it is hardly a tragedy.

8

Orgy

Pasolini thought highly enough of *Orgy* to choose it as the first of his plays to be produced for the stage in 1968. However, the critical response at the time was outright hostile. Tian called the play "a failed theatrical experiment" and most critics agreed ("'Orgia'"). Since that time opinion has largely reversed itself, and far from fading into obscurity, *Orgy* has instead received a considerable amount of both critical attention and praise.

The popularization of Genet and the Theatre of Cruelty in the Italian theatre, which occurred during the time which intervened between the first production of *Orgy* and the 1980s, is at least partly responsible for the change in attitudes toward the play. As Italian critics became more familiar with the theories of Artaud, they were provided with a context in which to place *Orgy*. Like Artaud, Pasolini sets out to "drain abscesses collectively." However, whereas Artaud depreciated the word and advocated working directly on the senses, Pasolini retains the word as the primary vehicle of his theatre, probably more so in *Orgy* than ever before. In contrast to Artaud, Pasolini uses words in *Orgy* to create images which work indirectly on the senses.

Although the relationship between Pasolini and the theories of Artaud is somewhat problematic, the similarities between *Orgy* and the theatre of Genet are unmistakable. Tian comments, "Here also certain moments seem to celebrate the same ambiguous theatrical rites celebrated by Genet, the exchange of roles of servant and master, of good and evil, of victor and victim" ("Nel cuore"). A sense of inversion permeates the work of both playwrights. The Man in *Orgy* realizes, "That / which we blaspheme is that to which we pray" (*Orgy* 140). Such a passage, attempting to prove the sacred by asserting the profane, could just as easily come from Genet.

However, Pasolini remains distinct from Genet in that, while Genet's characters sublimate themselves and achieve a sort of integra-

tion in their rituals and role-playing, Pasolini's characters do not. Instead, Pasolini continually exposes ritual and role-playing as an artificial
and therefore fallen reality, abandoning his characters to their sense of
irrevocable alienation. Pasolini despairs—where Genet has never really
hoped in the first place—of the restoration of an original self and an
original universe. Genet's characters assume that an autonomous God
does not exist so that they can then allow themselves to proceed to the
business of inventing Him in their own deviant way. Pasolini's characters refuse to accept His nonexistence, and this refusal impedes them
from inventing Him. Instead, they insist on rediscovering an original
God antecedent to their own powers of invention, who has been lost.
However, as Groppali observes, "The more God is sought out, the more
atheism affirms itself" (L'ossessione 52).

As a result, Orgy is probably Pasolini's most desperate and heartfelt
play. In it, Pasolini discards the ironic stance and Brechtian distancing
which had characterized his approach to his material in Pigsty. The
characters of Orgy, in contrast, are far from being caricatures, as Pasolini
immerses himself in their psyches more fully than in any other play.
The play recounts the story of a bourgeois couple who engage in sadomasochistic sexual rituals on a nightly basis. Eventually the Woman
decides to kill herself. The Man then attempts to revive these rituals
with the Girl, a young prostitute he has met. He ties her up and men-
aces her, but she escapes, naked. He then dresses himself up in her
undergarments, confesses to a repressed homosexuality, and kills himself.

The desperate sincerity of the play serves to highlight the hypocrisy
inherent within the theatrical medium itself, as characters are reduced
to describing in graphic detail the actions which the actors playing these
characters cannot actually commit onstage. The Man tells his wife, "I
want to *really* kill you. / I want to *really* die" (Orgy 134). His very insistence that what he does is real merely emphasizes that it is not, as the
audience is reminded of the disparity between the dramatic action onstage and the real situation it ostensibly would represent. Rinaldi com-
plains that "the protagonists . . . *are not giving a play*. In fact, everything
is based on the hypothesis of non-actualized theatre" (303). However,
this is precisely Pasolini's point, that theatre is by its very nature hypothetical and nonactualized. No matter how Realistic an aesthetic it may
adopt, its only true reality is as a system of signs which, at best, can
only indicate another reality with which it might be engaged, but from
which it is irreparably removed. Dramatic action may thus be viewed
as an artificial construct, not unlike the bourgeois universe, which is
fallen from the primal reality of which it is only a shadow. Conse-

quently, as a shadow of a shadow, stage activity devolves into a pathetic and hypocritical pantomime which Pasolini does not hesitate to eliminate from his theatre.

Although the theatre as a whole may remain an unreal fabrication, for Pasolini the words which constitute it do have their own more genuine reality. Rinaldi astutely notes that "the images of the orgy are the true reality" (302). Pasolini discards stage activity in favor of words as the most effective theatrical means of representation. Words function in *Orgy* much as they did in ancient Greek drama, describing perverse and extreme acts which Pasolini would not have hesitated to present in an immediate and visual way on film, but which would appear awkward and unconvincing onstage. In *Medea, A Thousand and One Nights* and *Salò*, Pasolini shows the dismembering of bodies in a graphic and immediate manner. In the "trilogy of life" films and *Salò* sexual scenes are also quite explicit. Even as early as *Accattone*, there is a strong sense of texturality and physical violence in Pasolini's cinema. In contrast to such physicality, the Man in *Orgy* can only *tell* his wife that he will bring workmen and boys to violate her and rape her without talking to her or kissing her. He can only *say* that he will mount her but ejaculate outside her in a position where she cannot see him. He can only *claim* to have knifed their elder son, to have drowned the younger, and to have thrown them both in a sack into the river. In similar fashion, the Woman can only *recount* her imminent suicide and her own plans to kill her sons, but none of this is ever shown.

As opposed to the catatonic reticence of Julian, the Man and Woman in *Orgy* are obsessed with verbal expression. Despairing of the possibility of resurrecting an original androgynous Father, they invoke Lacan's fallen "Law of the Father." In fact, for them, verbal expression assumes an almost therapeutic function. Barthes has argued, "Signification, in short, is the dialectical movement which resolves the contradiction between cultural man and natural man" (*Image* 27–28). As language eases the couple's pain of self-alienation, resolving the contradiction between their cultural and natural selves, it becomes ritualized into a poetic orgy of words, making the play Pasolini's most lyrically beautiful and haunting, the closest both in tone and imagery to his early Friulan poetry.

Rinaldi claims, "The theatre of poetry becomes poetry that destroys the theatre because it eliminates the physical dimension" (302). However, much of Pasolini's poetry, particularly in *Orgy*, is specifically oriented to creating the physical in words. The Woman's praise of male youth is little more than a listing of physical features:

How much love for this youth with sunken cheeks,
high cheekbones and sweaty forehead,
beneath the pink clay helmet of his short hair,
he watches me with his child's eyes,
he squints in the sun, his eyes like little slits. . . .
How much love for the dark youth,
who certainly comes from Sicily,
with his adolescent's mouth, mean
like a barbaric slave, but full of a mother's delicacy.

(*Orgy* 131)

Such passages of detailed description, particularly of young males, can be found throughout the plays. They reflect Pasolini's fragmentary *corps morcelé* aesthetic sensibility, as he dissects the human body, making fetishes of its various parts, and "fixing" on these parts with his verbal imagery. Such "fixed" passages of description are also analogous to Pasolini's long-held close-ups in film, wherein the camera seems to contemplate the physical reality before it. By using such a technique, Pasolini does not seek to disembody the physical so much as he attempts to read the language of physical reality as an expression of spiritual truths. In this context, the intimate camerawork of the entirety of *Teorema* comes to mind, as well as the extensive close-ups of Jesus in *The Gospel according to Matthew* and of Medea in *Medea*.

Like Pasolini's camera, the Woman in *Orgy* is adept at reading body language in this way. She tells the Man that the silence of those he brings to rape her will not deter her from knowing them:

They speak to me with the language of the flesh.
By the form . . .
the way . . . the time . . .
the intensity with which, entering inside me,
they make their long or brief confessions. . . .
From this I know their souls, their characters,
without need of words, in just a few minutes.

(*Orgy* 132)

She reads the book of the reality before her. In a similar manner, the Man reads the wounds he has inflicted on his wife as an expression of his desire to kill her and also as a sign of his own attraction toward death. The Man refers to body language as an "ancient language." It is a primal reality which cannot be alienated because the body is both signifier and signified. In contrast, verbal language appears as an artificial construct, removed from original reality, attempting to signify something other than itself. It is a product of man's alienation and self-consciousness. Santato aptly notes that "the body is the *real* sign, the only expression of reality that can confront the unreality of the word: reality expresses itself in and via the body." (275). The Woman realizes:

> Therefore our reality is not that
> which we express with our words,
> but that which we express
> via ourselves, using our bodies.

(Orgy 144)

The word retains its position as Pasolini's primary means of theatrical expression, but, paradoxically, it may do so only by taking a subservient role to physical reality and physical language, both of which it tries to recreate in verbal imagery.

As the body presents itself as the only real sign, the couple turns to sex to provide them with a sense of integration and a recuperation of the pre-fallen self. Sex offers them an escape from their social roles. The Man speaks of "the truest freedom: the same as that of the animals" (*Orgy* 104). The couple attempts to infuse sex with a religious significance. The Man describes orgasm as "an ecstasy in which the world disappears / and God begins to reappear" (*Orgy* 177). Although sex may be the vehicle of transcendence, the imagery Pasolini uses to describe it is neither romanticized nor prettified, but gritty and animalistic. Such imagery functions as a verbal correlative to the visual texturality of his films. For example, there are references in *Orgy* to the smell of urine and the stench of semen. At one point the Woman comments:

> The most filthy love,
> that is the only thing that, along with agony,
> is truly lost.
> Truly lost . . .
> because it is made of bodies that corrupt.

(Orgy 160)

Passages of this sort assert that any transcendence or recuperation of God which is achieved by sexual means is susceptible to the imperfect nature of man's animal self. In fact, a sense of physical decay pervades the play. The Man, a virtual hypochondriac, is obsessed with his ailments as proof that his fallen state is irreversible. His liver problems and the Girl's tuberculosis are signs to be read of their imperfection, decay and inevitable mortality.

The imperfection of man's body also manifests itself in its inability to maintain orgasm. There are no dreams of flight in the play. If the reappearance of God is made contingent upon orgasm, then He will remain elusive and not a permanent fixture of the universe. God appears only to disappear again, leaving the couple with an ever-greater sense of loss and an ever-greater urgency to recuperate themselves from their fall. The Man comments:

> The first time is not enough
> because you do not remember it. . . .
> And you never stop looking for it
> because we forget it every time. . . .
> Each new erection,
> or anxiousness, or guilt of an erection,
> wants to repeat it,
> wants God to return.
>
> (*Orgy* 175–76)

As transcendence is temporary, it becomes necessary to repeat the sexual act and to ritualize it. The nocturnal existence of the couple has thus evolved into a continual, ritualized search for this sexual retrieval of a primal, pre-fallen self and of a pre-fallen God.

Orgy is distinct from Pasolini's other plays in that it is the only one which focuses upon an active heterosexual relationship. For Pasolini, the heterosexual rites of *Orgy* do not constitute a union of sexual complements so much as an inextricably sadomasochistic conflict of sexual opposites. The play follows in the Strindbergian tradition with what Santato calls "the impossible coexistence between the two figures of the Man and the Woman" (277). Pylades sees himself in Orestes, and the Father in *Affabulation* sees himself in the Son, but the Man in *Orgy* does not see himself in the Woman. While homosexuality, as a form of secondary narcissism, attempts to view the world as an extension of the self, the heterosexuality of the couple in *Orgy* merely serves to confront them continually with the world as other.

Consequently, the "sexed partial beings" of the Man and the Woman view each other as objects, appropriating their animal selves in a conscious and deliberate manner. The Man tells her, "You are nothing else for me but a thing. / I do not recognize myself in anyone else" (*Orgy* 110). The Woman retorts, "You are nothing else to me but a means / that I've found . . . / for realizing my desire in my solitude" (*Orgy* 110). He cannot overcome her solitude, as neither can provide the other with a true sense of integration. Their sex degenerates into a power exchange not unlike that upon which bourgeois society itself is based. Their sadomasochism evolves as a natural consequence of this power relationship. Groppali calls their sadomasochism a reflection of "the organized disharmony of the cosmos" (*L'ossessione* 46).

Groppali argues that the Woman's "body is victim inasmuch as it concedes to the penetration of the phallus" (*L'ossessione* 61). However, Pasolini, like Strindberg before him, does not take such a simplistic view of the situation. The Woman in *Orgy* bears no resemblance to the more delicate and exploited Rosaura in *Calderón*. Instead, Pasolini unmasks the Woman's seeming passivity as the more profound and subtle form of power in the relationship, as she is a willful accomplice in her own degradation. She confesses, "He who possesses is innocent / he who is possessed is guilty" (*Orgy* 118). She is a succubus, a knowing parasite of her husband's libido. The Man refers to the Woman's "inhuman passivity . . . / in front of which my naive violence cannot resist" (*Orgy* 124). She is the inverse of the nurturing mother figure idealized by Pasolini in his Friulan verse and in his films *Mamma Roma* and *The Gospel according to Matthew*.

However, *Orgy* can be read from an entirely different perspective in which neither the Man nor the Woman plays a purely dominant role in the relationship. In fact, implicit in the play is a sense that power may not be hierarchical at all, but symbiotic. The French writer Michel Foucault has described "force relations which, by virtue of their inequality, constantly engender states of power" (*History* 92). The sadomasochism of the couple would thus seem situationally induced, a consequence of their fallen state of being, their lack of wholeness and consequent inequality. Foucault observes:

> Power is exercised rather than possessed; it is not the "privilege" acquired or preserved, of the dominant class. . . . Furthermore . . . power is not exercised simply as an obligation or a prohibition on those who "do not have it"; it invests them, is transmitted by them and through them. (*Discipline* 16–17)

Neither the Man nor the Woman really "possess" power. Instead, they symbiotically "exercise" it upon one another, as they passively allow it to "invest" them and be "transmitted" by them. Their passive acceptance of this power is actually a conscious, calculated decision, and Pasolini views it as being tantamount to the eating of the fruit of the tree of knowledge.

In fact, *Orgy* constitutes perhaps Pasolini's most virulent attack on passivity as complicity in evil, even more so than *Salò*. Nevertheless, the Woman attempts to defend her behavior and that of her husband, "But how can we free ourselves from this evil / if it is so infinitely more beautiful than every good?" (*Orgy* 144). Like that of Genet, the world of *Orgy* has been inverted by its universal fall from its primal state. Committing evil thus gives the couple the illusion that they are integrating themselves with a universe that is itself evil. In like manner the Girl falls victim to the Man in this inverted world because she is, as the Man maintains, "guilty of innocence."

For Pasolini, passivity is the opposite of what he terms "individuation," a process analogous to the American writer Ralph Waldo Emerson's concept of self-reliance.[1] "Individuation" refers to the evolution of a person as a specific spiritual-physical entity in the universe, as a distinct human manifestation of that universe. In contrast, passivity results in conformity, which is tantamount to self-negation. The couple's suicides are merely the culmination and climactic expression of the nihilism and self-negation of their previous conformity. The Woman refers to the "idiotic anticipation of a wretched death / committed in the name of the neighbors" (*Orgy* 160). Although the couple desperately attempts to resuscitate their primal, pre-fallen selves by means of their sexual rituals, the sadomasochistic turn these rituals take must eventually reveal itself as merely another manifestation of their irreversible self-destruction. Having sacrificed their original psychological-spiritual identities to their bourgeois roles, the sacrifice of their animal selves, their bodies, is inevitable. The critic Enzo Golino writes, "Death as the habit of repression . . . is the necessary consequence, the only way out of the social plague which encircles the protagonist" (*Orgy* theatre program).

Death presents itself as the only viable means of escaping the closure of the bourgeois universe, much as it did in *Pigsty*. Pasolini emphasizes this sense of closure in *Orgy,* as all the action in the play happens behind closed doors. The Woman is overcome with a sense of claustrophobia and suffocation. Her long suicide monologue concludes, "They'll say she died for a breath of air" (*Orgy* 164). Within this enclosed bourgeois universe all action is ephemeral or, at best, masturbatory, allowing for no real progress or movement. The Woman laments that "nothing moves here in this room. / Inside and outside, stillness" (*Orgy* 152). In such a fixed world, the couple is capable of only the nonaction of death.

Pasolini follows in the tradition of Maeterlinck and Strindberg by discarding a clearly defined sense of chronology, so that the sense of stillness in the play is compounded by a sense of timelessness. Within a hermetically enclosed universe, all events are foregone conclusions anyway. The Man's suicide may close the play but it is an event which actually occurred prior to the beginning of the play, as the Man declares in his opening monologue. Rinaldi notes, "From the beginning, the play develops in a posthumous time, on the other side of death, as if every-thing had already happened" (301). This sense of "posthumous time," of retrospection, contributes to the strong elegiacal lyricism of the play.

However, the first death the Man and Woman suffered was not their suicides, but the loss of their original selves as they fell into their adult bourgeois social roles. The Man's opening monologue is followed by a series of pastoral memories of the couple's youth, that period prior to their fall. These memories precede the couple's sexual rituals as a means of somehow recuperating the world and the God they have lost. They are ritualized in a verbal manner, giving Pasolini's poetry free rein. These memories do in fact provide an opening, albeit a temporary one, in the enclosed universe of the couple. The Woman notes, "They are like breaths of reality that manage to reach . . . / Where every wind has fallen" (Orgy 139). Unfortunately, life cannot be maintained as a mem-ory, and in the long run the couple's nostalgia for their previous exis-tence, like the temporary integration offered by orgasm, serves only to heighten their awareness of their present alienated condition and exile from Eden.

Dreams are even less effective than memories in providing the cou-ple with an escape from their society of alienation. In fact, the dream state eludes the couple. Instead of achieving the integration offered by sleep in Pylades and Calderón, the couple spends their nights awake, trapped in self-consciousness, so that almost every scene in Orgy takes place at night. The Woman is even an insomniac, who restlessly paces the hallways. She tells the Man, "But you forget we have always lived / pretending to dream" (Orgy 145). However, the Man does manage to achieve the integration of the unconscious state when he passes out in his own vomit after the Girl has fled. He describes his sleep:

> There was a concert of angels
> against the walls of my cranium.
> I listened to it with attention and rapture.
>
> (Orgy 182)

This experience confirms the Man in his aspirations toward a Lacanian "externalization of his desire," as in death he seeks to regain the rapture of unconsciousness on a permanent basis. He describes his imminent suicide as a dream from which he will not awaken.

The Man's suicide is foreshadowed by his murder of his two sons, Oedipal figures in their own right, who are also extensions of himself. Aged four and six years, the two sons never appear in the play, but they are described as versions of Pasolini himself and his younger brother, Guido. The Man talks about them to the Girl as if they were still alive:

> The elder is cruel,
> his eyes are full of love for his mother.
> The smaller one is also full of this same love,
> but his eyes laugh as if nothing matters to him:
> he is light-hearted and funny.
>
> (*Orgy* 167)

The quotation reflects the Oedipal tensions in Pasolini's own family, wherein the Laius father senses the threat his sons offer to both his authority and his place with the mother. Their power consists of their potential for developing a virility greater than their father's, a virility which will render him impotent as they replace him in the rite of kings.

Because of this the Man eventually perceives of them as the authority figures to be replaced. Such a conception also allows him to deny his own fall into the Laius role. He confesses, "Sometimes they seem older than me" (*Orgy* 167). *Orgy*, like *Affabulation*, thus presents an inversion of the rite of kings. The Man's phallic use of the knife in murdering his sons, again like that in *Affabulation*, emphasizes the inverted Oedipal nature of the killings. The Woman herself makes this inversion explicit when she speaks of "the son with pretensions of being a father / or the father who is still a son" (*Orgy* 163).

After his sons are killed, the Man becomes obsessed with the greater virility of the potential Oedipus figures of all males younger than he. He asks the Girl about her clientele, curious to hear about her latest encounter with a boy from the south doing his military service in Bologna, where the play is set.[2] The Man pictures the young soldier "with his large Sicilian member / strong as a trunk and tender as a fruit" (*Orgy* 173–74). Eventually, as in *Affabulation*, the Laius figure's inordinate interest in the more potent sexuality of the Oedipus figure reveals itself as repressed homosexuality. The Man confronts this homosexuality only a few moments before he commits suicide.

The Man's suicide is also the form the death of the prince takes in the play, as he is both father and son, oppressor and oppressed, Laius and Oedipus. On one hand, he is an Oedipus figure, seeking an opening in the universe. He claims, "I have remained this prepubescent boy just emerged from the larva" (*Orgy* 183). His adult bourgeois role has not totally absorbed his primal, Oedipal identity. It has not reduced him to a caricature as it has Klotz and Herdhitze in *Pigsty*. Nevertheless, he is also a Laius figure, a bourgeois who, by his own admission, has accepted "a small place in the world of power" (*Orgy* 186). As a Laius figure, he is destined to kill the Oedipus within him. The Man thus functions as the embodiment of the intestinal struggle of the bourgeoisie, an emblem of its self-destructiveness.

9

Beast of Style

The last of Pasolini's plays, *Beast of Style* was also the last to be produced, premiering in 1985. It has generally been considered the least theatrically effective of the plays, more schematic than dramatic. It is certainly the most loosely constructed of Pasolini's dramatic works, the most "open" in terms of plot, far removed from both the structural closure of *Calderón* and the more classical linear structure of *Affabulation* and *Pigsty*. Rinaldi calls it "a series of lyric confessions . . . a reconstruction of time past based on the archaic Friulan model" (312–13). Although quite different in tone, *Beast of Style*, like *Orgy*, is both an extension and a contamination of Pasolini's Friulan verse. In fact, the play becomes literature about literature. This extremely metaliterary nature of the play has led some critics to consider it Pasolini's worst. Groppali does not discuss the play in his book, and only Santato and Rinaldi addressed themselves to the text prior to its first stage production.

Beast of Style recalls the archaic Friulan model also in that it is highly autobiographical, much more so than any of the other plays. Pasolini himself wrote that "in fact, it is a sort of autobiography" ("Preface," *Beast*). Although Pasolini's life played an integral role in shaping the artistic sensibility that informs all his art, none of his novels written after the Friulan period nor any of his films could accurately be described as autobiographical. The autobiographical nature of *Beast of Style* at least in part accounts for Pasolini's reluctance to complete it. Writing over a period of eight years, he was continually adding and cutting scenes as his own life evolved. Eventually, in 1974, Pasolini made the arbitrary decision of concluding the play, even though his own life was to continue for another year and a half.

As an autobiography, *Beast of Style* is not a direct representation of Pasolini's life. Instead, he reflects his life in that of Jan Palach, a real-life Czech who immolated himself in protest against the invasion of Prague by armed Russian tanks in the summer of 1968. Although the real Jan

Palach was only a university student of typical college age in 1968, the life of Pasolini's Jan, like his own by that time, spans four decades. Pasolini begins his play in the 1930s with a youthful and idealistic Jan. Jan's interest in writing poetry in the dialect of his native province of Königgratz corresponds to Pasolini's own use of Friulan. Jan asks himself, "Poet of what? / Of my sex and of my country" (*Beast* 205). It is precisely this mixture of sexual and political consciousness which most characterizes Pasolini's work as well. Jan's contempt for the institutional education he received corresponds to Pasolini's for the University of Bologna. Jan claims, "I would have killed all the professors at the University of Prague / for a single verse by Rimbaud" (*Beast* 230). Similarly, Pasolini has also often cited Rimbaud as an important influence on his early poetry.[1] Like Pasolini, Jan is a homosexual who flees the provinces for the capital where he pursues a literary career. He wins the Stalin prize for poetry much as Pasolini had been nominated for Italy's prestigious Strega prize for literature.

Both Jan and Pasolini come from bourgeois families. Jan's is described as the richest and most highly esteemed in the town of Tabor. Similarly, Pasolini and his mother had been regarded with a particular deference and respect by the people of Casarsa in the Friuli, where they resided during the war years. However, Jan's mother is not a portrait of Susanna Pasolini, but the culmination of the fallen, unnatural mothers in *Orgy* and *Pigsty*. Jan's mother is a rigid and vehement fascist whose habitual drinking contributes to her frequent fits of temper. With this in mind, Rinaldi views her as "an exceptional expressionistic portrait of Carlo Pasolini" (316). Indeed, the character Karel even describes her as "dressed in a soldier's old uniform" (*Beast* 226). Conversely, Jan's father reflects the gentle and retiring nature of Pasolini's mother. While the femininity of Pasolini's mother dictated her submissive role in life, Jan's father is oppressed and victimized because he is Jewish. Jan does not have a younger brother, but he does have a younger sister who, however, is not so much a representation of Guido Pasolini as is Jan's childhood friend, Karel. Like Guido, Karel is the man of action who dies during the war while fighting for liberation.

However, as an autobiography, *Beast of Style* is not so much a catalogue of the events of Pasolini's life as it is an attempt to recount the development of his psyche, of his artistic sensibility, and of his intellect. His aim is not the specific, but the universal. Jan notes, "What happens here / in this country, in the center of Prague / is an index of what happens in the world" (*Beast* 244). Jan's tale of alienation thus becomes representative of the modern human condition in general. He is a sort of modern Everyman in search of his place in the cosmos. The allegorical characters of Capital and Revolution thus debate for Jan's soul at the conclusion of *Beast of Style* in much the same manner as man's soul was the object of contention in medieval morality plays.

Although the play can be viewed as a contamination of Pasolini's own autobiography, it is also indebted to Aeschylus and to Expressionist *Stationendramen*. Much like an Aeschylean tragedy, *Beast of Style* consists largely of monologues by the protagonist which are interspersed with choral passages. However, the episodic structure of the play is more reminiscent of Expressionist theatre. Like the Man in the German playwright Ernst Toller's *The Man and the Masses,* Jan is simultaneously a martyr for and at odds with the masses. He identifies himself as a Christ figure:

> I relive his condemnation for you,
> because I bleed from the cock and from the heart,
> while you belong to that species
> who stand beneath the cross.
>
> *(Beast* 200)

As Jan bleeds from his cock as well as his heart, Pasolini again explores sex as a vehicle for spiritual transcendence. In fact, the play opens with Jan masturbating in the woods, something which he does habitually. He calls the nonprocreative sex of masturbation "the mechanism which liberates the male" (*Beast* 199). However, the integration and liberation offered by sex cannot be maintained, and in the long run the temporary nature of orgasm serves only to increase Jan's sense of self-consciousness and awareness of his fall. He eventually discredits such an approach to transcendence, even interpreting the sexual impulse as a proof and manifestation of man's fall and mortality. He states, "I masturbated all afternoon / decided to die" (*Beast* 200).

Jan forsakes his pursuit of transcendence by means of sex, but not before he transfers it to his sister, introducing her to it in the form of a shared incestuous encounter. She views sex as a "source of happiness without end" (*Beast* 266). As a character, she is actually Jan's alter ego. Pasolini makes this explicit when she comments that "the doubling of the character into two characters / is the greatest of literary inventions" (*Beast* 268). Inasmuch as she is Jan's alter ego, she is also Pasolini's alter ego, and like Pasolini, she has numerous anonymous sexual encounters with a variety of partners.

However, Pasolini renounces sex as a method for achieving transcendence and integration not only in the character of Jan, but also in the character of Jan's mother. Her speeches parody the late Romanticism of Pasolini's Friulan style, substituting for its rarefied ethereal imagery the grotesque, and profaning what had been held sacred. She taunts Jan with the sordidness of man's animal nature, reveling in sex as a fall from or even a negation of the spiritual. The Madonna-and-child imagery of the Friulan verse deteriorates into a freakish celebration of the Oedipus complex. She tells Jan:

> You spilled out
> from this belly
> among the little bourgeois brats,
> and there you stayed . . .
> with the shit of Jews and the blood of queers.
> I strip in front of you, sonny boy,
> and yell out: Mount me, on top, fuck me,
> play with my tits, baby, come on
> and kiss me on the mouth, touch my belly,
> don't be afraid, give it to me, come on!

(Beast 253)

Exulting in her fall, she is a self-proclaimed Nazi, a comic version of the fascists in *Salò*. For her, Nazi atrocities merely constitute a gruesomely engaging game of survival of the fittest, another manifestation of man's attempt to submerge his divided self in his animal nature. She appears flanked by two pathetically emaciated concentration camp victims. The more formidable volume of her physical presence alone is enough to establish her power over them, rendering them her slaves. She describes them to Jan:

> Look at those two cocks dangling from their bellies.
> . . . His name is Bongo, while the first one
> is named Fido, just like our dog.

(Beast 254)

Instead of offering man a sense of transcendence, here his animal nature serves only to dehumanize him, reducing him to the level of dogs as in *Salò*.

Confronted with the failure of sex as a means of integration, Jan turns from being a poet of his sex into being a poet of his country. Like Pasolini, he becomes a communist, declaring himself a disciple of Lenin, an intellectual who fights for the poor and the oppressed. He believes that those who have no franchise in the bourgeois power system live in a sort of pre-fallen Eden, creating his own version of Pasolini's "peasant myth." As a poet of his country, Jan provides Pasolini with the opportunity to observe his own public image. This allows him to disarm his critics by engaging in a bit of self-effacing self-criticism of his own. It also permits Pasolini to demonstrate his own keen sense of self-awareness. A series of Jan's adversaries comment:

> KORNHAUSER: Intellectuals
>   invent swaggering
>   appeals
>   only in order to compensate
>   for their own personal
>   sense of loss
>   of social function
>   and of belonging
>   to the world of the masses.
> MANNHEIM: The ascetic fanaticism
>   of the intellectual
>   is the compensation for a
>   more fundamental
>   integration
>   with his social world. . . .
> VAN MISES: His passionate
>   antipathy against   .
>   capitalism
>   is only a pretext
>   behind which he covers his hate
>   for his colleagues
>   who have been more successful.

(*Beast* 214–15)

Such satirical self-criticism is reminiscent of Pasolini's treatment of the film industry in his film *The Ricotta* (1962; *La ricotta*), and of his amusing self-portrait as Chaucer in his film version of *The Canterbury Tales*.

In *Beast of Style* Pasolini continues in this critical vein to the point where he undermines the sincerity of Jan's political engagement and commitment. Santato comments that "the obsessive theme returns of the insurmountable dissociation that separates 'the diverse one' from history and the world" (290). Ultimately, Jan remains as alienated from the world as he is from himself. He is only an observer of, rather than a participant in, the cataclysmic historic events which occur in Czechoslovakia during his lifetime. Rinaldi claims that for Jan "history becomes poetry" (314). In fact, in a typically bourgeois manner Jan appropriates historic events as objects to be put to use, as raw material for his writing. He inadvertently admits as much when he reveals that his humanism, and by extension his communism and his entire political commitment, is contingent upon aesthetic concerns. He asserts:

> I am still one who,
> for pure aesthetic love
> and incestuous sensuality,
> considers the death of an individual
> to be intolerable, incomprehensible and identical
> to the death of all humanity.
>
> (*Beast* 223)

This is Jan's pompous and rather vacuous reaction to the slaughter which accompanied the German takeover of Czechoslovakia in 1939. Jan degenerates into an ivory tower poet, eventually disengaging his poetry from the world around him which he hollowly claims is his source of inspiration. He himself contradicts this claim when he asserts that "literature is impermeable / to that which is considered non-literary" (*Beast* 245). Accordingly, he dismisses the importance of the content and the message of his verse, and his literary efforts become a quest for style, as he himself confesses.

Style for Jan is no longer a matter of decoration, or accompaniment, or method; it becomes the very substance and content of his work. Removed from external influences and fallen from the primal, Jan's poetry becomes a closed system, as masturbatory as his escapades in the woods, as hermetic and artificial a construct as the bourgeois universe and the bourgeois sensibility which spawned it. It becomes metaliterary, as the signifier usurps the significance of the signified. As Jan becomes concerned with style, it is not what the word represents, but the choice of the word itself which is important, a choice made according to the aesthetic criterion as to how the word insinuates itself into the broader literary structure of his work as a whole. Rinaldi comments that Jan "makes the gesture of writing poetry rather than writing poetry" (316). The creative process, the gesture itself, becomes the artwork. Jan may not genuinely be either a poet of his sex or a poet of his country, but he does retain his identity as a poet. If nothing else, he is a poet of poetry.

In Pasolini's *The Canterbury Tales*, Chaucer eventually realizes that he writes for the simple joy of the story-telling process. In a similar manner, the act of poetry-making provides Jan with the sense of transcendence which neither sex nor political engagement could effectively give him. Like the dream process, poetry-making recreates the universe as an integrated whole in which the self and the world are one. Consequently, Jan views poetry as a manifestation of the divine, and the play includes long paeans as Jan praises Rimbaud, Mallarmé, Kafka, Dylan Thomas and numerous other writers whom he associates with literary hermeticism. He effuses:

> What will I be able to do in the shadow of these European gods. . . .
> Oh, I am not responsible for it!
> My immortality is justified by Theirs.
>
> (*Beast* 222)

However, Pasolini discredits the transcendence that is achieved by means of poetry-making. The immortality attained by Jan and his poetic predecessors is neither spiritual, nor existential, nor even physical. Instead, it is merely the social immortality offered by fame. Rinaldi has called Jan "an intellectual social climber" (315). Indeed, in his pursuit of fame as a poet Jan is only following in the bourgeois literary tradition, even as his poetic mentors were nothing more than the idols and perpetrators of bourgeois culture. The chorus describes Jan's readership not as revolutionaries but as "the petit bourgeoisie of Prague" (*Beast* 242). He cannot escape his bourgeois origins, and his espousal of communist ideology merely fulfills his function as "the degenerate son" in the intestinal struggle of the bourgeoisie. His mother deflates his self-delusions:

> It's not that my womb conceived
> a good communist
> but because my womb conceived a bad bourgeois.
>
> (*Beast* 257)

Instead of promoting revolution, Jan actually perpetuates the closure of the bourgeois universe by the very detachment of his left-wing rhetoric and his implicit support of the communist party power structure. Cherif, the director of the play's premiere production, notes, "It is the seduction that this system of power exercised upon him (and others) that leads him to deviate from the real" (*Beast* theatre program). Although Jan purports to play the Oedipal role and bring a new order, eventually he realizes that with his financial and critical success he has become a Laius figure. He admits that he receives the official approval of the Stalin prize for literature with "Pilate's hands" (*Beast* 251). At one point a group of rebellious youths, protesting the presence of the Russian military in their country in 1968, burn an effigy of Jan in defiance of the Soviet authority he represents. By naively failing to discern that the communist hierarchy is just another manifestation of bourgeois authority and closure, Jan has transformed himself from a Christlike martyr into a Pilate. In this way, *Beast of Style* also presents the death of the prince.

10

The Theatre of the Word in Production: A Practical Perspective

Although much of Pasolini's *Manifesto* is devoted to theory, he does provide some indications as to methods of production which might be suitable for his plays. The methods he advises are primarily aimed at combatting the Italian traditions of *mattatore* theatre and director's theatre. In contrast to conventional Italian practice, he primarily advocates the submission of the actor and the director to the demands of the text and the playwright.

To achieve this he proposes *"the almost complete disappearance of the mise-en-scéne . . .* all of which will be reduced to the indispensable" (*Manifesto* 134). In this manner he hopes to undermine the Italian directorial penchant for visualization. Instead, he wants to highlight the verbal element of his theatre. He views his theatre as "the text and the actors facing the public: an absolute parity between these two groups of interlocutors, who look at one another in the eyes . . . the scenic guarantee of a real democracy" (*Manifesto* 145). In this dialogue between the text presented by the actors and the audience, the role of the director, far from being an autocratic one, fades into relative unimportance.

However, Pasolini does not advocate the complete removal of the director from the Theatre of the Word. Nevertheless, he does limit his function to what has been called "making the truth live" (Mancini 115). Such a light-handed approach reflects the metatheatrical nature of Pasolini's theatre, that it is a representation of a representation already removed from primal reality. In such a theatre the director is not responsible for creating an expressive system of signs, but need only discover and "make live" the expressiveness already inherently within the systems of signs placed at his disposal (i.e., the text, the actors and the theatre medium itself). His production need not be informed by his own theatrical and artistic sensibilities, as it does not rely on either his creative or his interpretive powers. Instead, the production requires the "democratic" participation of Pasolini's audience, their contribution to the theatrical event and their reconstruction of the play in their own minds based on its presentation. In essence, the audience usurps the role of the director. This approach strikes at the core of the director's theatre which in Italy is virtually created by the director's personal artistic sensibility, whether he uses a text or not.

As with the director, Pasolini also seeks to subjugate the actor. The function of both is to present, not to represent or interpret, the theatrical text. Pasolini advises:

> The actor . . . *must simply be a man of culture.* . . . Therefore, he need no longer base his ability on his fascinating persona. . . . Instead, he should base his ability on his capacity truly to comprehend the text. He must not be an interpreter of who bears a message (theatre!) which transcends the text itself: he must be the living vehicle of the text. . . . He must render himself transparent to its thought. (*Manifesto* 142)

In contrast to the subproletarian actors Pasolini often used in his films, for his theatre he demands as an actor a select member of the bourgeoisie. Such a choice of actor helps to guarantee that the polemic of his text will be understood. It also emphasizes the intended democratic nature of his theatre, as both actors and audience come from the same social class.

For similar reasons, he also embraces the use of formal spoken Italian in his Theatre of the Word. He had rejected formal Italian in many of his films, preferring to use the colloquial *romanaccio* in *Accattone* and *Mamma Roma*. In *The Decameron* he used the Neapolitan dialect, so that the film had to be shown with accompanying subtitles even within Italy itself. However, the metalingual, literary nature of his theatre demands that "the theatre of the word . . . accept . . . conventionalized Italian" (*Manifesto* 139). In fact, "conventionalized Italian" was not artificial to the elite bourgeois members of his audience, nor is it inappropriate to the characters of his plays who are themselves bourgeois, unlike the protagonists of many of his films.

Interestingly, Pasolini wanted to ensure that the manner in which the language was presented not call attention to itself and detract from the content of the text. This may seem paradoxical inasmuch as the "content" of Pasolini's texts is in one sense the style itself, his self-conscious use of language. However, ultimately he was only concerned that his language maintain its aesthetic quality and not seem stilted, as it might in the mouth of an actor who was not "a man of culture." In any case, he advises, "The oral Italian of the texts of the theatre of the word must be assimilated to the point that it becomes real" (*Manifesto* 139).

The fact that the *Manifesto* includes suggested production practices confirms Pasolini's intention that his dramatic texts were meant to be performed, that he did not consider them to be closet drama. There can be no doubt that the plays were intended for the stage, as Pasolini himself directed a production of *Orgy*. The first of the texts ever to be produced for the stage, it premiered at the Deposito D'Arte Presente in Turin in November 1968.[1] The production received uniformly hostile reviews and Pasolini was accused of dilettantism. However, such a cold reception must be seen in the context of the Italian theatre of the time. With its minimal use of stage activity and emphasis on the word, Pasolini's production was in stark contrast to the experimental gestural productions of Memè Perlini and Giuliano Vasilicò which then dominated the Italian avant-garde theatre. As opposed to the displays of directorial visualization offered by Luchino Visconti and Giorgio Strehler in the commercial theatre, Pasolini's production was ascetic. His limited set was described as a mere "scenic box" (Rosati).

Nevertheless, Pasolini did make some concessions to the theatrical practices of his day, so much so, in fact, that the relationship between this first production of *Orgy* and the theories in the *Manifesto* remains problematic. Although Pasolini claimed to champion the word, he paradoxically underscored his production of *Orgy* with music. The use of music was and is a common practice in the conventional Italian theatre, a type of theatre with which Pasolini did not want his Theatre of the Word identified. However, by using music, he set a precedent which has persisted in most of the other productions of his plays that have since been mounted. Paolo Terni, who provided the musical selections for the world premiere production of *Beast of Style*, defends the use of musical accompaniment in performing Pasolini's theatre. Terni argues, "Pasolini's disdain for the Theatre of Chatter ... should be read also (and perhaps above all) from a musical point of view" (*Beast* theatre program). Terni's basic position is that musical accompaniment is only an extension of the musicality already within the lyricism of Pasolini's verse and that such accompaniment serves only to emphasize the abstract expressiveness of the verse. Admittedly, Pasolini was as much concerned with the aesthetic and musical qualities of his texts as he was with their ideology. However, precisely because his plays do have a musical quality, any use of musical accompaniment in producing them seems redundant.

Pasolini's production of *Orgy* diverged from the *Manifesto* also in his choice of theatre space and the audience this space entailed. The stated purpose of the Deposito D'Arte Presente was to function as "a free and cordial meeting place for people interested in the most current expressions of the arts" (qtd. in Radice, "'Orgia'"). This "meeting place" did not provide Pasolini with the select members of the bourgeoisie he sought to address as his audience. Instead, admission to the production was limited to a subscription audience of the Deposito itself. As the prerequisite for subscribing was more a matter of wealth than a sincere interest in culture, Pasolini's production of *Orgy* played to those same women in fur coats whom he had hoped to deter from his theatre by charging them thirty times the normal price of a ticket. Pasolini had unwittingly reduced the cultural rite of his Theatre of the Word to a social rite of the most conventional sort of elitism.

Despite the failure of this production of *Orgy*, Pasolini did receive offers to produce the other plays, most of which he turned down. However, in 1969 a production of *Pylades* was mounted at the Greek theatre in Taormina, Sicily, as part of Italy's summer theatre season. The theatre, with a view of the coast and Mount Etna as a backdrop, was a suitable "found space" for the play as a contamination of Greek myth. Nevertheless, the production was criticized for its lack of elaborateness and described disparagingly as a "lecture-oratorio" (Marzullo). Pasolini had planned to direct a more fully mounted production of *Pylades* as part of the regular theatre season at the Teatro Fenice in Venice in 1976, but the production was never realized due to his death. Since that time, probably because of its subject matter, the play has become something of a staple of the Italian summer theatre season which revolves around the use of the country's open-air Greco-Roman theatres.

Probably the most successful and popular production of *Pylades* to date was that directed by Melo Freni in the summer of 1981. In accord with Pasolini's theories, there was no set. This accommodated the production as it travelled from one place to another, playing in a variety of open-air theatre spaces. It also left the actors to perform in an "absolute void" which was suitable to the existential nature of the play. However, Freni's production did involve extensive use of lighting design. The rationale for such a scenic innovation can be easily found in the text of *Pylades*, as Pasolini dedicates many of the more poetic passages of the play to description of various types of light and their significance.

A director who had previously mounted productions of the poetry of Ezra Pound and Sappho at the Greek theatre in Syracuse, Sicily, Freni paid careful attention to the language of Pasolini's play. Despite his extensive use of lighting, Freni mounted a production which relied on the verbal rather than on the visual, on his actors rather than on his designers. Although all the leading actors received favorable reviews,

Ida Di Benedetto, one of Italy's best contemporary actresses, was particularly noteworthy as Electra. One critic wrote, "Di Benedetto (Electra) puts her experienced instinct to good use. . . . She is statuesque, obsessed and sensual, as is required" (V. R. G., "Dibutterà"). Such a performance is essentially within the Italian tradition of bravura acting. Di Benedetto's performance may have been at odds with Pasolini's theories, but not with the extraordinary demands of his text. The critic Lorenzo Bocchi justly views Pasolini as "a lyric author who considers the monologue to be the most theatrical of theatrical events." Indeed, Pasolini's long and "most theatrical" monologues are show pieces, hearkening back to the tradition of the operatic *recitativo*. As such, they virtually require a certain degree of bravura to make them effective in performance. Freni realized this and did not inhibit his actors from taking advantage of this opportunity to put their virtuosity not merely on display, but to good use.

The minimalistic approach used in the various summer productions of *Pylades* can in part be accounted for by the fact that they played in Italy's Greco-Roman theatres. This same minimalist aesthetic is often used when actual ancient Greek and Roman drama is performed in these open-air theatre spaces. However, the extreme minimalism of Beppe Navello's 1976 production of *Affabulation* and Lorenzo Salveti's 1982 production of *Orgy* stemmed solely from their desire to follow Pasolini's theories as closely as possible, even more closely than Pasolini did himself. Premiering less than three months after Pasolini's death, Navello's *Affabulation* was mounted in homage to its author. Navello made a sincere attempt to discard the superfluous spectacle of the Italian theatre and neutralize the scenic action. One description reads:

> Beppe Navello, the director of this *Affabulation*, seems to have applied the method originally described by the author almost to the letter. The public listened for two hours and hardly saw anything. The action was intentionally kept in check, blocked into rigidified schemes wherein the few gestures and scenic pieces seemed almost provocatorily disassociated from the development of the dialogue. (G. C., "Pasolini")

In Salveti's production of *Orgy* the audience was seated on benches in a rectangle. The scenery was simple, wooden, and painted white. The actors performed with script in hand, presenting the text to the audience in a manner that was in keeping with Pasolini's literal description of their function. They faced out toward the audience in an effort to make the audience's relationship with the word as direct as possible. Salveti, like Navello, was faulted for his slavish dedication to theories which most critics deemed impracticable. Although Navello's *Affabula-*

tion and Salveti's *Orgy* may have appealed to Pasolini purists, the integrity of these productions did little to establish Pasolini's reputation as a viable theatre artist.

The prominent director Luca Ronconi embroidered upon this minimalist aesthetic, expanding it to monumental, even operatic proportions in his 1977 production of *Calderón*. The epic nature of his approach to *Calderón* was reflected in his decision to mount the play together with Calderón's *Life Is a Dream* and Hugo von Hofmannsthal's *The Tower*. Inasmuch as these two texts are thematically related to *Calderón*, their production served to amplify the intertextual nature of Pasolini's play. As the first project of Ronconi's theatre laboratory at the Teatro Metastasio in the town of Prato, near Florence, this trilogy of plays was an ambitious choice.

Gae Aulenti, a noted architect, provided Ronconi with a set which respected Pasolini's disdain for the scenic element, while at the same time maintaining a sense of overall design and space conception. A platform was built out over the orchestra and auditorium, creating a large oval playing space and unifying the stage with the seating space. The result incorporated the audience, which was limited to some one hundred spectators at a time, into the playing area. This unification of space was in accord with the intended democratic nature of Pasolini's theatre. Furthermore, it drew the audience into the play in a manner reminiscent of Velazquez' *Las Meniñas*, the play, like the painting, functioning as a series of mirrors reflecting both inward and outward. As Pasolini indicates in the text of *Calderón*, figures based on those in Velazquez' masterpiece were flown and provided scenic background at various points in the play.

Velazquez' painting also provided the inspiration for the use of a large mirror at one end of the playing area, thereby increasing the sense of space, universality and void. A door frame, again like the one in the painting, was placed at the opposite end of the oval from the mirror and indicated the hope of an opening in the closure of the universe. Characters moved as elements within a void, unable to escape through the door. All movement was directed outward from the center of the oval, as if pulling against gravity. The circular patterns which resulted contributed to the sense of frustration and the inability to take action that characterize the play. Scenic pieces other than those mentioned specifically by Pasolini in the play were used, but these were kept to a minimum, either flown or carried on, so that the oppressive emptiness of the space predominated.

Costumes were also nonrealistic and minimalist, but, like the set, maintained a sense of concept and design. Rosaura was dressed in white, her family in black, and other characters were dressed in a neutral ochre in an effort to de-emphasize the spectacular. As with the set design, lines were kept simple and plain.

Ronconi developed a specific acting style for the play. The style, which has since been dubbed "Ronconian," has persisted in modified form in various productions of the Italian avant-garde and art theatre. Proponents of the style claim it is not a style at all, but only a method. This method attempts to counter the Italian *mattatore* tradition by emphasizing the demands of a specific text rather than the actor's persona as the primary and determining factor in creating a role for the stage. Consequently, it involves extensive textual study and analysis before any sort of traditional rehearsal process begins. Line readings are based on caesura, grammatical construction, syntax and word choice, rather than on the hypothetical psychological states of the characters. The acting process thus becomes more intellectual than inspirational.

This method, as first practiced in Ronconi's *Calderón* in its most extreme and rarefied form, resulted in an almost abstract acting style. In response to Pasolini's desire that the persona of the actor be subordinated to a comprehension of the thought of the text, Ronconi aimed at "a diction as impersonal as possible that puts in evidence the individual words, amplifying their meaning as much as possible . . . so that the only sense of what happens is the ideological" (Ronconi, qtd. in Cibotto, "Calderón"). The style that developed involved slow, dilated, almost monotone pronunciation which was accompanied by deliberate, dance-like movements. The actors performed in a highly stylized manner, reminiscent of accounts of early productions of Maeterlinck's plays, one thought process leading inevitably into another, as if they were in a somnambulant state or trance. The style, an attempt to come to terms with Pasolini's theories on acting and the word, proved to be more controversial than the theories themselves, and many critics mercilessly assailed it. Bonino, however, wrote more positively, "The acting is . . . anti-naturalistic . . . shattering the normality of everyday speech in order to substitute it with 'another syntax' which is more strongly communicative" ("Pasolini, Ronconi"). The style thus exposed rather than used verbal language as "the first social contract," penetrating beneath the artificial surface of realistic inflection in order to recapture some sense of original, pre-fallen, even abstract meaning in words.

Although the production could justly be described as an opera without music, it did not rely on the bravura of specific performers, as they all acted in a uniform style not based on the individuality of their personas. In fact, actors and roles were interchangeable, and the role of Rosaura was played by a different actress in each of the three sequences. Far from being *mattatori*, the actors were virtual "voluntary instruments in an almost scientific experiment" undertaken by the director (De Monticelli, "I tre sogni"). In any case, many of the actors were unknown at the time, so that Ronconi was the only real star of the production. Ultimately, he subjugated acting bravura at least as much with his own directorial bravura as with Pasolini's text. Consequently, Ronconi was probably more of a factor in the production than were Pasolini's theories. Although Ronconi may be faulted for turning the Theatre of the Word into a director's theatre, his production of *Calderón* can nevertheless be credited with garnering Pasolini's theatre a considerable degree of serious critical attention which it had not previously enjoyed.

While Ronconi responded to Pasolini's theories with the evolution of a distinctive and rarefied style, Giorgio Pressburger, in his 1980 version of *Calderón*, aimed at a more mainstream and accessible approach to the play. Pressburger incorporated the use of an acting style which gravitated toward the realistic, even the Stanislavskian, using verbal language as a "social contract." However, the play lacks in subtext, and such an approach made it seem shallow, as words failed to be appreciated for their own inherent value, something which Ronconi had stressed. In accord with both Realist and Italian tradition, Pressburger allowed his actors to exploit their personas in order to individualize their interpretations. However, only Paolo Bonacelli as Basilio managed to raise this more Realistic approach to the level of true bravura in a performance that Bonino described as a *"tour de force . . . in its use of cadence distilling the poetic intentions of Pasolini"* ("Pasolini, nei 3 sogni"). The choice of Bonacelli as Basilio was fortuitous as he had performed a similar role of a power figure for Pasolini himself in *Salò*.

Although Pressburger mounted a more conventional production, his *Calderón* did not become the popular success he had hoped. In Turin it was warmly received, but in Rome its reception was somewhat cool. In Vicenza at the Teatro Olimpico, it played to an almost empty house on opening night. The critical response ranged from grudgingly positive to indifferent, as the production was noticeably flawed by the glaring disparity between the nature of the text and the style of production. Pressburger had mistakenly sought to play allegory as reality, to discard the poetic in favor of the prosaic.

This tendency became even more pronounced in Pressburger's film version of the play, wherein he attempted to concretize the imagery of Pasolini's verse, imagery which is often abstract. Like his stage production, Pressburger's film of *Calderón* was not a great success. Lacking in originality, Pressburger's film mimics and quotes Pasolini's own cinematic language. In the film of *Calderón* there are walking scenes on the periphery of the city, reminiscent of *Mamma Roma* and *Hawks and Sparrows* (1966; *Uccellacci e uccellini*). King Basilio's dwarves are dressed as angels, a quotation from the conclusion of *The Decameron*. The feces in Rosaura's cell in the mental ward calls to mind images from *Salò*. Rosaura herself is presented as a Christ figure with wounds pierced in her sides and nail punctures in her ankles, much like the protagonists in the conclusions of *Mamma Roma* and *The Gospel according to Matthew*. An approach as derivative as Pressburger's could not but result in an artistic failure. Consequently, the film of *Calderón*, like Pasolini's film of *Pigsty*, was static and flat, pointing up the great differences between Pasolini's theatre and his cinema. Unfortunately, the failure of the cinematic version of *Calderón*, again like that of *Pigsty*, has only served to discourage theatrical productions of the text from which it was made.

Where Pressburger failed to reach a mass audience, Vittorio Gassman succeeded. His two versions of *Affabulation*, the first in 1977 and the second in 1986, have proved to be the most popular productions, with both critics and audiences, of any of Pasolini's plays. In fact, the 1977 production bordered on becoming a cult phenomenon, as many of the young audience members returned on successive nights to see it again and again. Pasolini himself had realized that, because of the universality and clarity of its message, *Affabulation* would probably be the most popular of his plays. However, Gassman guaranteed the accessibility of the play to a mass audience by producing it fully within the Italian *mattatore* tradition. In direct opposition to Pasolini's *Manifesto*, Gassman was not so much a vehicle for the play as the play was a vehicle for him. In true *mattatore* style, Gassman was both director and leading actor in both the 1977 and the 1986 productions. On both occasions, critical response was overwhelmingly positive, directing itself almost entirely to Gassman who was credited with overcoming the difficulties of a problematic text. One critic asserted, "Gassman has worked miracles" (Vignorelli). Gassman, however, did not so much overcome the difficulties of the text as he avoided them.

Gassman's productions of *Affabulation* encouraged the absorption of Pasolini's theatre into the bourgeoisie by transforming it into a social rite, rather than mounting it as the cultural rite Pasolini had intended. Certainly the audience I saw at the Teatro Pergola in Florence in 1986 was not the select group of the bourgeoisie prescribed in the *Manifesto*.[2] Instead, the audience consisted of those "who attend the urban theatres and never miss a major Strehler, Visconti or Zeffirelli premiere," precisely those elements of the bourgeoisie Pasolini sought to exclude from productions of his plays. Attending Gassman's 1986 production of *Af-*

fabulation was a social event. In fact, it was *the* event of the 1985–1986 Italian theatre season. For months prior to the 1986 premiere Gassman engineered a relentless media blitz to promote his work. Interviews with Gassman appeared in such sensationalistic commercial magazines as *Oggi* and *Gente*. (In format and content these publications fall somewhere between the American periodicals *People* and *The National Enquirer*.) However, what was most unsettling about Gassman's production was not that it was a commercial venture, but that it was marketed as an example of serious theatre, sincerely engaged with the polemic of Pasolini's text.

In addition to his marketing techniques, Gassman secured the success of his social event by carefully editing the text in order to make it more palatable to his mass audience. Ronfani comments, "The text has been polished, purified, cleaned by Gassman" ("Dolce"). Such an approach is in direct conflict with Pasolini's own doctrine of contamination. Claiming to be in service to Pasolini's text, Gassman actually violated it, reducing it and neutralizing its virulence as he "polished, purified, cleaned" it of its homosexuality. In fact, any hint of the homosexuality which is so integral to the action of the play was virtually absent from Gassman's production. Gassman prudishly asserted, "Even the most driven scenes are represented with decency" (qtd. in Tumbarello 88). In contrast, Pasolini had never been so squeamish about the acceptance of his work as to tailor or otherwise compromise his artistic output. Another violation of the play came in the form of Gassman casting his son, Alessandro, in the role of the Son in the 1986 production. The casting aided Gassman in his media blitz, and much was made of its contributing an added dimension to the metatheatrical nature of the text, underscoring the Oedipal tensions of the play as father and son played father and son. As an important part of the social rite of Gassman's production, Alessandro's performance was well-received by critics and young girls hounded him for his autograph. However, Alessandro virtually yelled all his lines and, taken out of the context of the social event of the play, his performance was an embarrassment.[3] In any case, Alessandro totally lacked the haunting unearthly quality that Luca Dal Fabbro had in his performance of the Son in Gassman's 1977 version of *Affabulation*.

Although the actors in the 1986 version generally received more critical attention than their 1977 counterparts, both productions belonged to their *mattatore*. Gassman's was hailed as a "historic performance" (Lucchesini, "Nel nome"). Gassman himself asserted, "From the moment the curtain rises I am the protagonist" (qtd. in Tumbarello 88). In accord with *mattatore* tradition, Gassman subordinated everything to the protagonist in his 1986 version by viewing the entire play as a projection of "the great delirium" of the Father. This provided the rationale for the doubling of the roles of the Father and the Shade of Sophocles, both played by Gassman, and the doubling of the roles of the Mother and the Fortune-teller, both played capably by Paila Pavese.

Gassman and his cast as a whole wisely avoided the incongruous Realism that had marred Pressburger's production of *Calderón*. A seasoned veteran of poetic drama, Gassman gave the poetic language of Pasolini its due emphasis. However, Gassman's approach came more from the classical tradition of poetic drama rather than from any sort of post-modernist metalingual sensibility. Gassman essentially played Pasolini as he had played Alfieri, Manzoni and Shakespeare, relying more heavily on technique than on instinct for his *mattatore* bravura. He explains, "Taking up *Affabulation* again, I maintained the same attitude of humility I had the first time, as an interpreter of the word: rather than being theatrical, I had to control, control, control where I would have liked to give the gas" (qtd. in Lucchesini, "Pasolini e l'ombra"). Actually, Gassman's best moments were when he abdicated this feigned humility, gave the gas and immersed himself and the audience in his own bravura, connecting with Pasolini on this level. The "Paternostro" and the long speech which follows the Father's killing of the Son were particularly gripping, as Pasolini's "most theatrical" monologues again lent themselves well to the Italian bravura acting tradition.

The set designs for both Gassman's 1977 and 1986 productions could best be labelled a sort of suggested Realism. Tian describes Gabriele De Stefano's design for the 1977 production as "little more than a tracing of objects and figurative lines" ("Conversazione"). The one-set scene design with which Gianni Polidori provided Gassman in 1986 was perhaps more carefully thought out, as Gassman took more time in preparing this second production of the play. Bonino writes:

> A scene design of high, clear abstraction, intensely symbolic: the villa of the Father, a magnate in the Brianza, is a stage within a stage, with white gangways and automatic moving parts, and it is also something of the mythic Theban palace with its snow-white stumps of columns: by any account, it was far from an environment of naturalistic verisimilitude. ("Gassman padre e figlio")

Polidori used geometrically pure shapes painted a uniform white for set pieces. These cones, spheres and cubes delineated the space, while at the same time leaving the actors alienated by the starkness of their environment. Guido Baroni's lighting, at times itself white, enhanced this effect. The lighting played an integral role in the lovemaking scene between the Girl and the Son, as they were seen in silhouette from behind a white screen, in accord with Gassman's dictum on decency.

The 1985 world premiere production of *Beast of Style* was called "a titanic, monumental project" (Garrone). Cherif, its director, basically followed in the tradition of operatic minimalism established by Ronconi in 1977 with *Calderón*. However, Cherif attenuated this style, making it more accessible. His main concern was that the polemic and musicality of Pasolini's poetry receive their due emphasis, rather than using the play as a pretext for displaying his own directorial bravura as Ronconi had done.

Marisa Fabbri was primarily responsible for disseminating the Ronconian acting method to the rest of the cast. She had formerly worked with Ronconi as an original member of his theatre laboratory in Prato. Together with Cherif, she evolved a less-rarefied version of the acting style used there. The actors in *Beast of Style* were taught to exploit the musicality of Pasolini's verse as a means of enhancing rather than obscuring its polemic. Consequently, the elongated, almost monotone pronunciation used in Ronconi's *Calderón* was discarded in favor of a performance style that accentuated the musicality of the language. Cherif's production thus became more of a spoken opera than Ronconi's had been. However, the method was still more intellectual than intuitive or emotional, as all line readings were based upon a structural analysis of the text and Stanislavskian techniques were cast aside. In accord with Pasolini's *Manifesto*, the actors considered their primary responsibility and function to be the presentation of this text, subordinating their own personas to its demands.

Davide Riboli as Karel was particularly adept at exploiting the emotional appeal of the poetic structures of Pasolini's verbal imagery. He allowed the polemic of the play to use the word, through the imagery it creates, to work indirectly upon the senses of both the audience and himself. His performance was a grotesque, hauntingly Expressionistic fusion of Italian bravura acting and the Ronconian analytic method.

Marisa Fabbri offered an even more impressive synthesis of these two traditions in one of the most riveting performances of the 1985–1986 Italian theatre season. In true Italian style, she did not hesitate to take full command of the stage, but she used Pasolini's words and polemic to do so. Bonino writes, "Marisa Fabbri . . . ignites a vein of grotesque irony: her twenty minutes are, as always, great theatre bordering on the greatest virtuosity" ("Pasolini si specchia"). Certainly the "most theatrical" monologue of Jan's Mother returning from the depths of hell to haunt her son benefits from such virtuosity and even requires it. However, if Fabbri's was a virtuoso performance, it was because hers was first a virtuoso analysis of the text, its polemic and its musical structure.

Unlike Fabbri, Maurizio Donadoni as Jan totally ignored the sense of irony with which Pasolini treats his character in the text. Donadoni mistakenly played Jan not only in full earnest, but also for a fully earnest reaction in the audience. Furthermore, instead of connecting with the musicality of Pasolini's verse as an expression of its polemical content, Donadoni's performance at times degenerated into mere sing-song and vocal histrionics—an ever-present danger with this sort of acting style. Admittedly, Jan is the most difficult role in any of Pasolini's plays. As such, it requires a degree of acting bravura and intellect which I felt Donadoni sorely lacked.

Although Cherif's *Beast of Style* was closely attentive to the verbal element of the play, the production was also strongly visual. However, the set and costume designs of the noted fashion designer Nicola Trussardi were probably as much a determining factor in this regard as was Cherif's direction. Inasmuch as the play spans a period of four decades and has changes of scene ranging from the Bohemian woods to Moscow, a Realist approach would have proved impractical at best. Instead, Trussardi turned to Expressionism, viewing the stage as a projection of Jan's mind, "a depository, a memory of history" (Trussardi, *Beast* theatre program). In fact, the production included many of the defining characteristics of Expressionism, as costume lines were distorted, lighting was harsh and sometimes angular or from the side, and the chorus was often used to form abstract geometrical patterns as if they were automatons.

Trussardi stressed the idea of the universality of the play, leaving the stage as an open space "where the actor, with his physical presence and the word, was capable of changing the geography and atmosphere without limitation" (Trussardi, *Beast* theatre program). The use of the cyclorama, like the use of the mirror in Ronconi's *Calderón*, increased the sense of space and void, a void which Jan desperately tries to fill with his poetry-making. Also reminiscent of Ronconi's *Calderón* was the limited use of set pieces and the predominance of neutral colors. Cherif and Trussardi, however, punctuated the climactic moments of *Beast of Style* with splashes of bright red and deep blue.

Although Cherif aimed at making Ronconi's operatic mimimalism more accessible, his approach could not completely overcome the relative inaccessibility of the play itself. Consequently, although the production did receive favorable reviews and its style was deemed suitable to the text, it was not a popular success. In fact, the audience I saw was small and the production played for only a limited run in both Rome and Prato. Nevertheless, the audience in Rome was attentive and appreciative, apparently composed mostly of those select members of the bourgeoisie for whom Pasolini had intended his theatre.

Mario Missiroli's 1984 production of *Orgy*, which was revived during the 1985–1986 season, posed a compromise solution between the demands of accessibility and the peculiarities of Pasolini's dramatic text.[4] While Missiroli's production was distinctively his own, his approach resulted in a sort of hybrid style which incorporated elements of both the Ronconian tradition and the more conventional Italian theatre. The production was palatable enough to become both a critical and popular success, while at the same time maintaining a sense of artistic integrity. It did not deteriorate into a social rite, nor was it conceived as one. Unlike Gassman, Missiroli did not deem it necessary to tailor his production to public taste in order to transform the play into a successful evening of theatre. Instead, he included the integral nudity of the Man and the Girl that the text of *Orgy* requires at the end of the play. This created a highly effective moment of theatricality that addressed the very same obsessive bourgeois concern with "decency" and conformity that Gassman had allowed to shape his productions of *Affabulation*. Nevertheless, the nudity in *Orgy* did elicit some nervous laughter from a small part of the audience and some critics faulted Missiroli for using it.

However, on the whole Missiroli was credited with a successful production. His direction was strong, but, like Cherif, he essentially did not use Pasolini's text as a mere vehicle for his own directorial bravura. Bonino discerningly notes that Missiroli created "moments of intense visualization . . . without abdicating the uninterrupted narrative flow" ("'Orgia'"). Missiroli aimed at providing physical and visual images which were a suitable accompaniment to the text, rather than trying to physicalize the images of the text in a literal manner as Pressburger had done. Furthermore, Missiroli was careful that his visual images supported rather than intruded upon Pasolini's verbal images. His primary concern remained the extraction of the high theatricality of the long monologues of the play, as he knew full well that this is what makes Pasolini's theatre dramatically effective and viable.

Although Missiroli's work was admirable, Enrico Job must be credited with what may very well be the best scene design to date for a Pasolini play.[5] Job's costume designs were Realistic modern dress, but his set defied Realism in the extremeness of its high-tech austerity. The design stressed plasticity and asceticism, creating a sterile, clinical environment of slick surfaces. The couple's bedroom was oppressively

grand and sleek, the color of nickel. The absence of windows contributed to the sense of claustrophobic closure in the play, making the
bedroom seem more like a prison. The overall effect was more sugges-
tive than suggested, in contrast to the designs for Gassman's two versions of *Affabulation*.

Franco Nuzzo used a film noir–type lighting which rendered the
surfaces even more austere and hard. Only the scene that occurs at
dawn was given a sense of warmth, illuminated by a rose-colored wash.
In general, lighting was stark, with high contrast of highlight and
shadow. Actors often appeared in silhouette. Forming patterns of light
and shadow against the hard smooth surfaces of the set, their physicality was emphasized to the point where at times they appeared as mere
objects on the stage. Side-lighting was used extensively and blackouts
punctuated the end of each episode, much like the closing of a camera
shutter.

In order to exploit the theatricality of the monologues of the play,
Missiroli allowed his actors to indulge in their own bravura. Laura Betti,
probably Pasolini's closest friend during his lifetime, repeated her 1968
role as the Woman in Missiroli's production. The Woman's suicide
monologue is one of the best in Pasolini's plays and Betti did not hesitate to take advantage of its "most theatrical" nature. Her Woman was
a sort of modern-day Lady Macbeth, driven to distraction by the immobility of her world. Her bravura was not merely a display of fiery temperament, but moderated by her professionalism, experience, instinct
and personal commitment to Pasolini's polemic. Except for the suicide
scene, her interpretation of the Woman, like that of the servant Emilia
in the film *Teorema*, was relatively contained and haunting in its contain-
ment.

Alessandro Haber gave a somewhat subtle but nevertheless strong
performance as the Man. His bravura manifested itself as "a texture of
neuroses continually on the verge of lacerating into a *raptus* . . . a great
performance maintained between clinical abstraction and the tremors
of the pain of his alienation" (Ronfani, "Crudele"). Haber made a deceptive use of understatement, painfully detached and ironic. He presented
the Man as a primal human furtively struggling against the automaton
which threatens to subsume him, a man trapped in his own internal
monologue.

From the critical and popular failure of Pasolini's 1968 *Orgy* to the
critical and popular success of Missiroli's 1984 *Orgy*, the contemporary
Italian theatre is gradually coming to terms with Pasolini's plays and
Manifesto. To a certain extent, Ronconi can be seen as attempting to
exaggerate the peculiar nature of Pasolini's theatre and transform it into

an avant-garde Theatre of Gesture or Howl. Pressburger attempted to ignore the peculiar nature of this theatre and turn it into a Theatre of Chatter. While Ronconi opted for what he considered to be artistic integrity, Pressburger sought greater accessibility and a mass audience. Directors and actors have continued to confront this problem of striking a balance between artistic integrity and accessibility when mounting productions of the Theatre of the Word. When integrity is a determining factor and the *Manifesto* is taken literally, the Theatre of the Word deteriorates into little more than a reader's theatre, as in Salveti's *Orgy*. When a premium is placed on accessibility and acceptability, the Theatre of the Word degenerates into a social event, as in Gassman's *Affabulation*.

Directors such as Cherif and Missiroli have aimed at avoiding these polar extremes. They have synthesized production styles which have taken into account the theories of the *Manifesto*, while at the same time not hesitating to incorporate practices from the conventional Italian theatre which benefit the texts. Their hybrid approach has allowed them to make use of both designers for visualization and acting bravura for verbalization. They have enlisted both design and bravura in an effort to encourage the imagery of Pasolini's verse to work indirectly on the senses and intellect of his audience. Such an approach may compromise the letter of Pasolini's *Manifesto*, but it need not compromise its spirit. As long as directors, actors and designers are willing to subordinate their talents to the demands of the Theatre of the Word, it will survive. Because of the quality of the texts, it may even thrive.

The Theatre of the Word as Post-Modernist Theatre: A Sociopolitical Perspective

There has been a predominant tendency to consider Pasolini's plays from a literary rather than from a theatrical standpoint. Admittedly, to a certain extent Pasolini does follow in an Italian literary tradition—that of the "high" Italian theatre which has always concerned itself with literary values. In this context, Enzo Siciliano, Franco Grassi, Ferdinando Camon and Alberto Moravia, to name only a few, have compared Pasolini's work favorably with that of Gabriele D'Annunzio. In their respective halves of the twentieth century, both Pasolini and D'Annunzio functioned as the social and political conscience of the country. The style and artistic sensibility of the writings of both reveal the evolution of a late Romantic tradition which is not entirely dissimilar. Using this tradition as a point of departure, both writers confronted the often anti-Romantic philosophical, political and aesthetic ideologies of the twentieth century, synthesizing their own frequently uneasy solutions. However, whereas D'Annunzio exalted nationalism and the glory of *patria*, Pasolini cried out against fascism as dehumanizing. While D'Annunzio believed in the cultivation of the individual *Übermensch*, Pasolini sought the primal and the original in the subproletariat masses. Finally, D'Annunzio championed the resurgence of the Italian cultural identity, while Pasolini could only lament its gradual disappearance in the face of commercialization and neocapitalism.

As Tian has pointed out, Pasolini's Theatre of the Word can also be seen "as the modern correlative of the tragic theatre of Vittorio Alfieri" ("Conversazione"). Indeed, both Pasolini and Alfieri attempted to reinterpret the ancient Greek rite of kings in a way that reflected the societies in which they lived and the conceptions of God and universe upon which these societies based themselves. Both of them created a polemical, even politically agitational, theatre. At the same time, they both sought to revive the beauty of the Italian language as it was used in the theatre by refusing to compromise the aesthetic quality of their texts. Unfortunately, Tian's observation may perhaps be most astute in that, although Alfieri's plays have endured to enjoy great critical acclaim, they have never become a staple of the Italian stage. The same fate may await Pasolini's plays as well.

However, Pasolini was not merely following in the tradition of D'Annunzio and Alfieri. His theatre remains distinct from theirs not only because it was written in a different time period, but because it was based on an entirely different conception of the medium of theatre itself. Pasolini was not simply trying to resuscitate verse drama. On the contrary, he was not attempting to make theatre poetry, but to make poetry theatre. This accounts for the particular tension between the lyric and dramatic forms in his work, between the personal and the public, between the psychological and the political. He uses a private sensibility (the lyric) to approach a social art form (the dramatic). He exhumes the inner workings of the psyches of his characters so that he can then extrapolate on the social and political significance of their behavior. As Pasolini's psychological-lyric method is subjugated to his the political-dramatic intent, the innate individuality of his characters is sacrificed again and again to the external forces which shape their identity. The English critic Gatt-Rutter claims that "these plays in fact fail to sustain free selfhood against . . . historical process" ("Pasolini," in Caesar 154).

Pasolini was in a distinctive and even privileged position to witness the effect of the "historical process" on man, as during his lifetime Italy made the cataclysmic transition from a basically underdeveloped country with a wealthy elite into the seventh most industrialized and richest nation in the world. Pasolini observed the progress of Italy's postwar economic boom as a materialistic illusion which actually served only to perpetuate man's fall. This progress de-spiritualizes man by placing him in a world which is quickly disintegrating from its original and primal wholeness, replacing it with an increasingly hermetic and artificial power structure. In any case, Pasolini saw that those in power benefited far more from progress than did the poor. Neocapitalism merely transformed the laborer into a consumer, neutralizing him, absorbing his desire for revolution and confirming him more than ever before in his subservient social role. The lower and oppressed classes are lulled into complacency and passivity by radio, television and advertising, the new opiates of the people of a consumer society. Pasolini saw consumerism as simply a more sophisticated, insidious and profound form of the same oppression that those disenfranchised from the power system have always suffered. He noted:

The needs induced by old capitalism were basically similar to man's primary needs. On the other hand, the needs which neocapitalism can induce are thoroughly and perfectly useless and artificial. . . . It must be added that Consumerism can create unmodifiable social relationships by establishing, in the worst case, a new technofascism or, as is more likely, by evolving a context of hedonistic ideology, false tolerance and . . . the false realization of civil rights. (qtd. in Adornato 123)

As consumerist society evolves, it becomes more and more removed from the original, from the animal and the spiritual, reducing man to a programmable object. Man creates an identity for himself by imaging himself in products, a process which contributes to his profound sense of self-alienation. Ultimately, he is robbed of self-determination, as those with power manipulate and even control his desire to consume. Camon observes that "the bourgeois state in the consumer phase perpetuates itself with the technology of persuasion, making its citizens believe that it functions to serve them while they sacrifice their lives to its deceptive value system." In essence, man loses his identity, as he sells his soul for material goods.

Interestingly, in his plays Pasolini examines this process as it manifests itself not in the lower classes, but in the bourgeoisie. His bourgeois characters tenuously delude themselves that they have kept their identities intact, that they remain the captains of their souls. However, the plays illustrate that any single individual has at best only "a small place in the world of power" and is no match for the system as a whole. Theodor W. Adorno of the Frankfurt School asserts that "the individual . . . has fallen behind the state of technology and become historically obsolete . . . he becomes the custodian of truth, as the condemned against the victor" (129). In effect, consumer society demands the death of the integrity of the individual. As Pasolini's protagonists strive for such integrity, they cannot avoid committing suicide of one form or another.

Pasolini's plays were fostered in a cultural and literary environment which was concerned with how best to counter the dehumanizing processes of the neocapitalist power structure. Eco, the left-wing critic Fortini and the avant-garde writers of the *Gruppo '63* censured the characteristic neo-realist use of simple description in addressing social injustices for reproducing linguistically the very same system it sought to combat politically. Ragusa observes, "The writers of the *Gruppo '63* were convinced that . . . the literature of the future would be marked by experimentation with form and not with subject matter" (240). As neo-realism had already liberated formerly taboo subjects (e.g., poverty, crime, etc.), it was now time for experimentalism to liberate form. In essence, an analogy was drawn between linguistic-literary structures and the sociopolitical structure of the neocapitalist world as a whole. As a result, the neo-realist acceptance of conventional linguistic-literary structure was interpreted as an acceptance, or even an affirmation, of the conventional power structure. In contrast, disorder or innovation in the linguistic-literary system was tantamount to revolution in the neocapitalist system. Consequently, literature was no longer called upon to describe or attack verbally, but to demonstrate and sabotage structurally.

The *Gruppo '63* member Edoardo Sanguineti, in particular, advocated a new hybrid of linguistic hermeticism which would take into account the literary sciences of structuralism and semiotics. In a manner reminiscent of Lacan, Sanguineti claimed, "The experience of words conditions (precedes) that of things" (qtd. in Wagstaff, in Caesar 39).[1] Supporting this approach, Eco has argued that "to change semantic systems means *to change the way in which* culture 'sees' the world" (*Theory* 274). According to this theory, the choice of signifier can change the very nature of the signified. This change does not merely affect how the signified is perceived—this would be simple Expressionism—but how it is conceived. In essence, Sanguineti's argument is that a rose by any other name would *not* smell as sweet. Extending this Lacanian notion into a political context, he asserted that linguistic structures carry with them a tacitly assumed ideology which is projected upon the world in order to make it comprehensible. In fact, Sanguineti called language "reality-as-ideology-would-have-it" (40). By changing language, the writer changes ideology; by changing ideology, the writer changes reality. Revolution thus becomes possible at the metalingual level. Pasolini adopts just such a metalingual method in his theatre as he attempts to effect social and political change.

However, Pasolini himself was somewhat distrustful of the literary sciences of semiology and structuralism, as they neglected the question of value and reduced everything before them to the level of phenomena. Although a synthetic semiological approach may be the only really savvy one in an information age, it is also by nature amoral, something which Eco has gradually come to realize in his own writings on semiology. It remains essentially hermetic, self-referential, based on the assumption that the relationship between signifier and signified is basically arbitrary.[2] Consequently, its engagement with social and political issues is tenuous. Indeed, despite himself, at times in his plays Pasolini delights in the hermetic beauty of his language to the extent that he neglects his sociopolitical agenda. Although *Beast of Style* in particular addresses this danger, all the plays are marked by a noticeable tension between hermeticism and social engagement, vacillating between the two.

Some Italians jealously guard Pasolini as something of a national treasure, seeing in his work a curious mix of Catholicism and Gramscian communism that is peculiarly Italian. However, the cultural concerns and literary sensibility which informed his work have since become as universal as his subject matter. The terms "hegemony," "structuralism" and "semiotics" have long since been disseminated among the intelligentsia of the English-speaking world to the point where they have become virtual buzzwords.[3] In any case, if Pasolini's theatre has not yet achieved overwhelming success in Italy, it may be because his plays belong more fully to a body of world theatre. Like Pirandello and Ugo Betti before him, Pasolini may first have to establish his reputation as a dramatist outside Italy before he can be canonized as a theatre artist on the Italian stage. He himself realized this: "It is true that I am writing something for the theatre in something of a strange manner, but I think it would be difficult to entrust it to Italian actors. I am thinking of translating it into English or French and letting them produce it in their countries if they want" (qtd. in Auglas 6). In fact, in the beginning his theatre received more critical attention abroad than in Italy. *Affabulation*, for example, was produced in Austria and France before it was ever a success on the Italian stage. Canali reports, "By 1975, while his theatre was being studied in France, in Germany, and even in the Soviet Union, we in Italy were still asking ourselves whether it was 'theatrical' or not" (51).

Indeed, Pasolini's theatre came at a time when theatre in Italy was either traditionally commercial or avant-garde experimental. He attempted to transcend the polarity of this theatre dialectic, even as his characters attempt to escape the Oedipus-Laius dialectic. He created a theatre which was neither conventional nor anticonventional, but rather what Eco might call "contraventional." Barthes writes, "The *contemporary* problem is not to destroy the narrative but to subvert it; today's task is to dissociate subversion from destruction" (*Image* 64). *Calderón* is a prime example of a subversion of conventional dramatic structure, while *Pigsty* constitutes a somewhat less-successful attempt at a subversion of conventional dramatic dialogue, verging on a built-in obsolescence of its own verbal code. Pasolini realized that destroying old conventions merely resulted in the establishment of new ones. Such a tactic would have eventually created a conventionally anticonventional avant-garde theatre, a trap he wished to avoid. Instead, his approach to the artistic medium of the theatre remained subversively contraventional.

The critic Todd Gitlin provides a definition of post-modernism which echoes Pasolini's own theatre aesthetic. Gitlin writes, "Post-modernism . . . is indifferent to consistency and continuity altogether. It self-consciously splices genres, attitudes, styles. It relishes the blurring or juxtaposition of forms. . . . It disdains originality and fancies copies, repetition and the recombination of hand-me-down scraps" (35). In essence, Pasolini was writing post-modernist theatre before the term *post-modernist theatre* was ever used in common parlance. In fact, his theatre shares common ground with the work of a number of theatre artists working a generation after him. Like Peter Brook in his production of *Orghast* for the Persepolis Festival in Iran in 1971, Pasolini views spoken language as already inherently metalingual, an artificial construct to be invented. Like Lee Breuer, Pasolini borrows from Eco's concept of the allusive "open" work, challenging preconceptions as to the nature and function of a theatrical text. Both writers contaminate their dramatic works with personal memories and intellectual references. Pasolini's doctrine of contamination is itself not dissimilar from the intertextuality of Heiner Müller's plays. For example, *Calderón, Affabulation* and *Pylades* virtually require an audience familiar with *Life Is a Dream, Oedipus the King* and the *Oresteia*, respectively. In much the same manner, Müller's *Hamletmaschine* and *Quartet* benefit greatly from prior knowledge of Shakespeare and *Les liaisons dangereuses*, respectively. Like Robert Wilson, Pasolini presents an evolution of the Artaud tradition of "draining abscesses collectively," as both he and Wilson attempt to expose and work upon the unconscious levels of human behavior. Whereas Wilson addresses his audience in an almost exclusively visual manner, Pasolini, at least in theory, addresses his audience in an almost exclusively verbal manner. Also in the Artaud tradition, the constant trading off and interplay of power roles in *Orgy* calls to mind not only Genet, but also the work of Fernando Arrabal. However, despite the sense of the symbiotic, all-absorbing nature of power which underlies *Orgy*, and, to a certain degree, all of Pasolini's plays, he does not forsake his desire to create a politically engaged theatre. Like Edward Bond in England and Franz Xaver Kroetz in Germany, his personal contact with the oppressed subproletariat determined the agenda of his theatre, an essentially political and social agenda. In response to this agenda, also like Bond and Kroetz, his texts are characterized by a rarefied use of language and an atavistic sense of violence. In any case, the parameters of what is considered "theatrical" and "untheatrical" in the post-modernist world theatre have been expanded far beyond the bounds the Italian critics set for the Italian theatre in the 1960s. Canali argues in favor of Pasolini's theatre finding its place in such a diverse body of world theatre:

How could or can a criticism as divided and sectionalized as the Italian ever truly comprehend in a complete manner a body of work as universal and eclectic as that of Pasolini? Or would it not be necessary to be born in a foreign country in order to better liberate this universality from the slag of its various contingencies and its Italianate-ness? (51)

An argument can be made for the relevance of Pasolini's theatre to American society in particular. Long a proponent of capitalism, America on the whole has been a forerunner in the evolution of a consumer society. Because American folk culture was more shallowly rooted than the more historically embedded folk cultures of Italy and Europe, consumerism has encountered less resistance here as it has attempted to replace cultural values with commercial ones. The so-called American yuppie phenomenon of the 1980s merely represents the consumerist society in its most advanced state of development to date. Young enterprising Americans, many of them from the labor classes, aspired to "a small place in the world of power" only to discover, like Pasolini's protagonists, that they had no real power at all. Ultimately, the yuppie phenomenon represents only the evolution of a more highly paid working class. Eco notes, "Faced by the prospect of a . . . network that expands to embrace the universe, every citizen of the world becomes a member of the new proletariat" (*Travels* 136). In this context, the yuppies basically became the supreme victims of a consumerist society, deceiving themselves that the material goods which function as the emblems of power in such a society actually offered them this power.

Believing power to be hierarchical, yuppies have scaled the social ladder only to discover that power may actually be what Foucault calls "massive" in nature. The concept of social mobility thus becomes obsolete. Eco explains, "Never created by an arbitrary, top-level decision, Power lives thanks to thousands of forms of minute or 'molecular' consensus" (*Travels* 175). This is particularly true of a modern democracy with a laissez-faire economy. Basically, however, Foucault's and Eco's observations merely speak to Pasolini's own indebtedness to the concepts of Gramsci regarding the symbiosis of power. Gramsci described

the "spontaneous" consent given by the great masses of the population to the direction imprinted on social life by the ruling class, a consent which comes into existence "historically" from the "prestige" (and hence from the trust) accruing to the ruling class from its position and its function in the world of production. (*Prince* 124)

In any case, the yuppie phenomenon can be viewed as the American version of the traditional bourgeois tendency to imitate the old aristocratic classes. Despite their persistent belief in social mobility, most Americans would recoil at the idea of being called "bourgeois" and there is a telling avoidance of the use of the term in this country. Like the term "elitism," the term "bourgeois" is a dirty word in a country which is democratic, and therefore mistakenly believes itself to be egalitarian. While democracy offers an illusion of egalitarianism, capitalism creates a society which appears as a hierarchy. In fact, ideologically, American society is profoundly bourgeois, based upon a belief in private ownership and private enterprise, and founded on the very premise of the separation of church and state that encouraged the bourgeoisie to flourish in the first place. As such, American society functions as the virtual bourgeois archetype of Pasolini's theatre.

Although Pasolini's Theatre of the Word is not by any means a cure-all for the ills of a modern neocapitalist society, it is working and will continue to work its way into the body of post-modernist world theatre. It has, since his death, escaped from the stigma of experimentation and dilettantism that led to its early obscurity and neglect. Nevertheless, its reputation in Italy remains controversial. Groppali comments, "On first sight the theatre of Pasolini seems to be a secondary activity in his overall body of work, and even one of secondary quality" ("Il teatro" 4). In Italy, this attitude has prevailed, as many critics have continued to ignore his theatre in favor of his films, poetry and novels. The problem is that despite the efforts of many of Italy's most prominent theatre artists, the Italian theatre has not gotten far beyond its "first sight" of Pasolini's work as a dramatist. However, this situation is changing as the quality of the plays and the sincerity of his engagement guarantee that their production is persistent, if still somewhat too infrequent. However, it should be kept in mind that Pasolini was not trying to reach a mass audience, but preferred the advanced groups of the bourgeoisie which would allow him to eschew the many Italian theatrical conventions for which he had such disdain. In any case, as Pasolini's plays transcend the specifics of time and place in which they were conceived, I believe his theatre will eventually surface as a very important body of dramatic work. Canali is even more enthusiastic in her praise. She asserts, "Pasolini's theatre . . . will be recognized as a masterpiece" (51).

Appendix

List of Productions

The list below includes all Italian productions of Pasolini's plays during the period 1968–86. However, there have been productions of Pasolini's theatre outside of Italy which are not included in this list.

Orgy. Premiered November 1968 at the Deposito D'Arte Presente, Turin. Directed by Pier Paolo Pasolini. Produced by the Teatro Stabile of Turin. Set design by Mario Ceroli. Music by Ennio Morricone. Cast: Laura Betti (Woman), Luigi Mezzanotte (Man), Nelide Giammarco (Girl).

Pylades. Premiered August 1969 at the Greek theatre, Taormina, Sicily. Directed by Giovanni Cutrufelli. Produced by the Compagnia Siciliana del Teatro Nazionale. Set and costume design by Nicoletta Sivieri. Music by Romolo Grano. Cast: Annibale Ninchi (Pylades), Arnaldo Ninchi (Orestes), Claudia Giannotti (Electra), Giuseppe Liuzzi (Old Man), Maria Estella Di Carlo (Woman), Bruno Cattaneo (Peasant), Vanda Vismara (Athena).

Affabulation. Premiered on 6 October 1973, at the Schauspielhaus Vereinigte Bühnen, Graz, Austria. Translated by Heinz Riedt. Directed by Peter Lotschak. Set and costume designs by Gian Maurizio Fercioni. Cast: Gerd Rigauer (Shade of Sophocles), Hannes Riesenberger (Father), Barbara Petritsch (Mother), Bernd Jeschek (Son), Hannes Schütz (Priest), Erika Deutinger (Girl), Ruth Birk (Fortune-teller).

Affabulation. Premiered on 30 January 1976, at the Cabaret Voltaire, Turin. Directed by Beppe Navello. Produced by the Compagnia del Teatro Proposta. Set design by Roberto Ambrosoli. Costume design by Guido Cherici. Cast: Aldo Turco (Father), Gisella Bein (Mother), Luca Bosisio (Son), Teresa De Sio (Girl).

Affabulation. Premiered on 22 February 1976, at the Espace Cardin, Paris. Translated by Jean-Pierre Burgart. Directed by Peter Lotschak. Set and costume designs by Gian Maurizio Fercioni. Cast: Akonio Dolo (Shade of Sophocles), Michel Auclair (Father), Judith Magre (Mother), Jean Louis Manceau (Son), Eleonor Hirt (Fortune-teller), Jean Reney (Priest), Nicole Derlon (Girl).

Calderón. Premiered May 1977 at the Teatro Metastasio, Prato, Italy. This same production was presented again the following year. Directed by Luca Ronconi. Set design by Gae Aulenti. Costume design by Gian Maurizio Fercioni. Cast: in the first sequence, Gabriella

Zamparini (Rosaura), Miriam Acevedo (Stella), Carla Bizzarri (Doña Astrea), Edmonda Aldini/Anita Laurenzi (Doña Lupe), Mauro Avogrado (Manuel), Giacomo Piperno (Sigismondo), Franco Mezzera (King Basilio); in the second sequence, Edmonda Aldini (Rosaura), Miriam Acevedo (Carmen), Giancarlo Prati (Pablo); in the third sequence, Nicoletta Languasco (Maria Rosa), Miriam Acevedo (Agostina), Franco Mezzera (Basilio), Mauro Avogrado (Manuel), Odino Artioli (Pablo).

Affabulation. Premiered November 1977 at the Teatro Tenda, Rome. It then moved to the Teatro Manzoni in Milan and the Teatro Alfieri in Turin. Directed by Vittorio Gassman. Set design by Gabriele De Stefano. Music by Fiorenzo Carpi. Cast: Vittorio Gassman (Father), Corrado Gaipa (Shade of Sophocles), Silvia Monelli (Mother), Luca Dal Fabbro (Son), Vanna Polverosi (Fortune-teller), Roberta Paladini/Laura Tanziani (Girl).

Calderón. Premiered March 1980 in Pordenone, Italy. This production then toured throughout Italy. Directed by Giorgio Pressburger. Produced by the Teatro Stabile of Trieste. Set design by Sergio d'Osmo. Cast: Francesca Muzio (Rosaura/Maria Rosa), Carmen Scarpitta (Stella/Carmen/Agostina), Paolo Bonacelli (Basilio), Gianni Galavotti (Sigismondo).

Affabulation. Premiered January 1981 at the Teatro dell'Elfo in Milan. It then moved to the Teatro degli Infernotti in Turin and the Teatro Goldoni in Venice. Directed by Angelo Savelli. Produced by the Cooperativa Pupi e Fresedde. Cast: Antonio Piovanelli (Father), Ivan De Paola (Shade of Sophocles), Fabienne Pasquet (Mother), Carlo Nuccioni (Son), Stella Del Prete (Girl). This production was noted for its emphasis on music and gesture, and for its attempt to present the play from the perspective of the Son rather than that of the Father. It also illustrated the importance of the verbal element in producing the Theatre of the Word, as the company hailed from Sicily and was criticized throughout northern Italy for poor, incomprehensible diction.

Pylades. Premiered at the Teatro Benevento, near Naples, on 18 July 1981. This production then toured throughout Italy. Directed by Melo Freni. Cast: Ida Di Benedetto (Electra), Luigi Mezzanotte (Pylades), Franco Interlenghi (Orestes), Mario Maranzana (Peasant), Marina Ruffo (Servant), Maria Teresa Sonni and Simona Caucia (Chorus).

Pylades. Premiered the summer of 1981 at the Teatro Grande, Pompeii. Cast: Barbara Valmorin (Electra), Michele Placido (Pylades), Guido Leontini (Old Man).

Orgy. Premiered April 1982 at the Teatro all'Orologio in Rome. Directed by Lorenzo Salveti. Music by Paolo Terni. Cast: Brizio Montinaro (Man), Maria Grazia Grassini (Woman).

Orgy. Premiered on 21 November 1984, as part of the Festival d'Automne dedicated to Pasolini, in the Grande Salle of the Centre Pompidou, Paris. This production then moved to Turin, and was revived again for the 1985–86 theatre season at the Teatro Argentina in Rome. Directed by Mario Missiroli. Produced by the Teatro Stabile of Turin and the Associazione "Fondo Pier Paolo Pasolini." Set and costume designs by Enrico Job. Lighting by Franco Nuzzo. Music by Ennio Morricone. Cast: Laura Betti (Woman), Alessandro Haber (Man), Daniela Vitali (Girl).

Beast of Style. Premiered November 1985 at the Teatro Valle in Rome and then moved to Prato. Directed by Cherif. Produced by the Associazione Fondo Pier Paolo Pasolini. Set and costume designs by Nicola Trussardi. Music by Paolo Terni. Cast: Maurizio Donadoni (Jan), Marisa Fabbri (Jan's Mother), Daniela Margherita (Jan's Sister), Davide Riboli (Karel), Mario Toccacelli (Novomesky).

Affabulation. Premiered on 23 January 1986, at the Teatro Manzoni in Pistoia, Italy. It then moved on to the Teatro Pergola in Florence and toured throughout Italy into the 1986–87 theatre season. Directed by Vittorio Gassman. Set design by Gianni Polidori. Lighting by Guido Baroni. Cast: Vittorio Gassman (Father/Shade of Sophocles), Paila Pavese (Mother/Fortune-teller), Alessandro Gassman (Son), Giusi Cataldo (Girl), Sergio Meogrossi (Priest).

Notes

Chapter 1

1. All translations are by the author of this text unless otherwise indicated.

2. Similarly, for Pasolini, Provençal and Catalan were the natural Oedipal counterparts of the more official Laius languages of French and Spanish, respectively.

3. Groppali's *The Obsession and the Phantasm: The Theatre of Pasolini and Moravia* (1979; *L'ossessione e il fantasma: Il teatro di Pasolini e Moravia*) was the first book dedicated to a study of Pasolini's theatre. Unfortunately, like many Italian critics, Groppali is more interested in formulating his own theories than in providing any sort of detailed textual analysis of the plays. Furthermore, the book completely neglects the plays *Pigsty* and *Beast of Style*.

4. Umberto P. Quintavalle has published a disturbing article ("Pasolini e i giovani di strada," *Il Resto di Carlino* 3 February 1976) in which Pasolini claims to have "experimented" with violence in his trysts with young boys so as to study their reactions. Pasolini, in a sociobiological manner, blamed the increasingly violent behavior of Italian youth on their lack of sexual abandonment. In any case, Pasolini seemed to view his patronage of the less fortunate subproletariat youth of Rome as his birthright, as with his financial power he "turned bodies into things."

5. Pelosi served a ten-year prison sentence for the killing.

Chapter 2

1. Although Pasolini capitalizes the various "rites" of the theatre he mentions in his *Manifesto* (e.g., SOCIAL RITE, CULTURAL RITE, POLITICAL RITE, etc.), these terms will hereinafter be left in lower case letters when used in this text unless in quotation.

Chapter 3

1. *Storia Interiore*, or *Nel '46!*, has still not been published.

2. Although the *Manifesto* was first published in *Nuovi Argomenti*, this text refers to a version published in the book *Il Sogno del Centauro*.

3. With the publication of her book *Pier Paolo Pasolini* in 1982, Friedrich became the first

English-speaking critic to address Pasolini's theatre. Her work contains one chapter devoted to a discussion of both the *Manifesto* and *Orgy*.

4. Pasolini had a particular disdain for the work of Giorgio Strehler. He commented, "Strehler . . . cultivates a form of contemporary academism I don't like. In my opinion he has codified a sort of theatrical kitsch" (*Centauro* 130). Consequently, it is not surprising that Strehler has never produced any of Pasolini's plays.

5. The characters in Pasolini's neo-realist novels who attend the cinema usually do so either to "make out" with their girlfriends, or to "roll queers" for money. Seldom do they ever have a genuine interest in watching the film.

6. A more detailed discussion of Eco's concept of the "open" work can be found in his "The Poetics of the Open Work," published in his book *The Role of the Reader* (Bloomington: Indiana University Press, 1979). This tract, with some variations, was originally published in Italian as *Opera aperta* (Milan: Bompiani, 1962).

7. An interest in the pastiche form and the beginnings of a post-modernist sensibility can also be found in Italian painting of the post-war era. The long undervalued late works of Giorgio de Chirico are basically reworkings of past models. For example, de Chirico's *Capriccio Veneziano alla Maniera di Veronese* (1951) foreshadows the appropriation of classical, Baroque and mannerist iconography found in the work of the post-modernist Italian painters Sandro Chia, Francesco Clemente and Carlo Maria Mariani in the 1980s. Like de Chirico, Pasolini was essentially "ahead of his time" in his attempt to bring such an aesthetic to the theatre.

Chapter 4

1. Pasolini's treatment of *Las Meniñas* in this play calls to mind the Irish painter Francis Bacon's reworkings of Velazquez' portrait of Pope Innocent X. I am unsure as to whether or not Pasolini was aware of Bacon's work, though it is entirely possible. In any case, it is not surprising that Pasolini would create a pastiche of a painting in light of the fact that he had also worked as a painter and had originally intended to write his university thesis on the iconoclastic Italian Baroque painter Caravaggio. Furthermore, the visual compositions of many of the scenes in his films are indebted to a variety of Italian Renaissance painters, such as Giotto, Masaccio and Piero della Francesca.

2. This connection between orgasm and flight permeates vernacular language and slang. In English we refer to the male genitalia as a *cock* or *pecker*, and have the expression "to flip someone the bird," while in Italian they use the words *bird* (*uccello*) or *feather* (*penna*) to designate the penis. Consequently, when Maria Rosa claims that her daughter Carmen's "feather is crumpled," the phrase takes on added meaning in Italian.

Chapter 8

1. It is doubtful that Pasolini was familiar with the works of Emerson, as Emerson remains a relatively unknown author in Italy, despite the fact that he once lived there. Nevertheless, the two writers do have some points in common. For instance, Pasolini's Romantic assertion that "only his eyes remained" for contemplating Nisiuti (see chapter 1) brings to mind Emerson's concept of the large eye which is so at one

with the world that only its capacity for vision distinguishes it as an entity separate from the world.

2. As Pasolini associated the Friuli region with his mother, he tended to associate the city of Bologna with his father.

Chapter 9

1. The importance of the influence of Rimbaud on Pasolini's poetry should not be trivialized. However, the relationship between the verse of Pasolini and that of Rimbaud is a topic unto itself and goes beyond the bounds of this study of Pasolini's theatre.

Chapter 10

1. An appendix at the end of this book contains a more complete listing of productions of Pasolini's plays than is presented in this chapter.

2. I personally attended performances of Gassman's 1986 *Affabulation*, Missiroli's *Orgy* and Cherif's *Beast of Style*, as well as rehearsals for *Beast of Style*. In addition, I saw Pressburger's film of *Calderón* and Jancso's documentary film of Ronconi's *Calderón*. All other assessments of productions in this chapter are based solely upon reviews, articles and interviews.

3. Nevertheless, Gassman defended the nepotism of his choice, "Alessandro is the right age and has the right physique. . . . Alessandro is a revelation" (qtd. in Tumbarello 88). Actually, Alessandro's gangling, awkward, adolescent movements did not correspond to the "bull" of a young man described by Pasolini in his play. As Alessandro is dark-haired, the ethereal blondness of the Son's hair, to which many of the more poetic passages of the text are dedicated, came from a peroxide bottle. In contrast, Dal Fabbro was a natural blond.

4. Missiroli is an experienced veteran, having been head of the Teatro Stabile of Turin for eight years, 1976–1984.

5. Enrico Job is probably best known for his set and costume designs for the films of his wife, Lina Wertmüller.

Chapter 11

1. Christopher Wagstaff's "The Neo-avantgarde," published in Caesar, provides a concise, clear discussion of Sanguineti's theories. These theories originally appeared in Sanguineti's *Ideologia e linguaggio* (Milan: Feltrinelli, 1965).

2. The arbitrariness of the relationship between the signifier and the signified has been with semiotics since its inception. Ferdinand de Saussure, generally considered the father of modern semiotic linguistics, took just such a stance in his landmark book, *Course in General Linguistics* (1916).

3. Richard A. Schweder provides an insightful and witty analysis of the trendiness of scholarly thought in his article, "In Paris—Miniskirts of the Mind," *New York Times*, 8 Jan. 1989, Book Review Section, 1, 28–29.

Works Cited

Books

Adorno, Theodor W. *Minima Moralia*. Trans. Edmund Jephcott. London: NLB, 1974.

Barthes, Roland. *Image, Music, Text*. Trans. Stephen Heath. New York: Hill and Wang, 1977.

Barzini, Luigi. *The Italians*. New York: Atheneum, 1967.

Caesar, Michael, and Peter Hainsworth, eds. *Writers and Society in Contemporary Italy*. New York: St. Martin's, 1984.

Carotenuto, Aldo. *L'autunno della coscienza*. Turin: Boringhieri, 1985.

Clark, Barrett H., ed. *European Theories of the Drama*. New York: Crown Publishers, 1978.

De Mauro, T. *Linguaggio e società nell'Italia d'oggi*. Turin: RAI, 1978.

_____ . *Storia Linguistica dell'Italia unita*. Bari: Laterza, 1976.

De Santi, Gualtiero, et al., eds. *Perchè Pasolini*. Florence: Guaraldi Editore, 1978.

Di Giammarco, Rodolfo. *Prima del Teatro*. Pisa: Teatro di Pisa, 1985.

Eco, Umberto. *The Role of the Reader*. Ed. Thomas A. Sebeok. Bloomington: Indiana University Press, 1979.

_____ . *A Theory of Semiotics*. Ed. Thomas A. Sebeok. Bloomington: Indiana University Press, 1976.

_____ . *Travels in Hyperreality*. Trans. William Weaver. San Diego: Harcourt Brace Jovanovich, 1986.

Foucault, Michel. *Discipline and Punish*. Trans. Alan Sheridan. New York: Random House, 1979.

_____ . *The History of Sexuality*, Vol. I, *An Introduction*. Trans. Robert Hurley. New York: Pantheon, 1978.

Freud, Sigmund. *Leonardo da Vinci*. Trans. A. A. Brill. New York: Random House, 1947.

Friedrich, Pia. *Pier Paolo Pasolini*. Boston: Twayne, 1982.

Gramsci, Antonio. *The Modern Prince and Other Writings*. Trans. Louis Marks. New York: International Publishers, 1968.

Groppali, Enrico. *L'ossessione e il fantasma: Il teatro di Pasolini e Moravia*. Venice: Marsilio, 1979.

Lacan, Jacques. *Écrits: A Selection*. Trans. Alan Sheridan. New York: Norton, 1977.

Luzi, Alfredo, and Luigi Martellini, eds. *Pier Paolo Pasolini*. Urbino: Argalia, 1973.

Mancini, Michele, and Giuseppe Perrella, eds. *Pier Paolo Pasolini: Corpi e Luoghi*. Rome: Theorema edizioni, 1981.

Maraini, Dacia. *Fare teatro: Materiali, teste, interviste*. Milan: Bompiani, 1974.

Pacifici, Sergio, ed. *From Verismo to Experimentalism*. Bloomington: Indiana University Press, 1969.

Pacuvio, Giulio, ed. *Cinquant'anni di Teatro in Italia*. Rome: Carlo Bestetti Edizioni d'Arte, n.d.

Pandolfi, Vito. *Teatro Italiano Contemporaneo 1945–1959*. Milan: Schwarz, 1959.

Pasolini, Pier Paolo. *Affabulazione, Pilade*. Milan: Garzanti, 1977.

———. *Amado mio*. Milan: Garzanti, 1982.

———. *Calderón*. Milan: Garzanti, 1973.

———. *Descrizioni di descrizioni*. Turin: Einaudi, 1979.

———. *Empirismo Eretico*. Milan: Garzanti, 1972.

———. *Il Sogno del Centauro*. Ed. Jean Duflot. Rome: Riuniti, 1983.

———. *Il sogno di una cosa*. Milan: Garzanti, 1978.

———. *I Turchi in Friuli*. Munich: Istituto Italiano di Cultura, 1980.

———. *La Nuova Gioventù*. Turin: Einaudi, 1975.

———. *Pier Paolo Pasolini: Le poesie*. Milan: Garzanti, 1975.

———. *Porcile, Orgia, Bestia da Stile*. Milan: Garzanti, 1979.

———. *Teorema*. Milan: Garzanti, 1968.

———, trans. *Orestiade*. By Aeschylus. Turin: Einaudi, 1960.

Rinaldi, Rinaldo. *Pier Paolo Pasolini*. Milan: Mursia, 1982.

Roncaglia, Aurelio, et al. *Per Conoscere Pasolini*. Rome: Bulzoni & Teatro Tenda, 1978.

Santato, Guido. *Pier Paolo Pasolini: Opera*. Vicenza: Neri Pozza Editore, 1980.

Siciliano, Enzo. *Alberto Moravia: Vita, parole, e idee di un romanziere*. Sozogno, Milan: Gruppo Editoriale Fabbri-Bompiani, 1982.

———. *Pasolini*. Trans. John Shepley. New York: Random House, 1982.

Stack, Oswald. *Pasolini on Pasolini*. Bloomington: Indiana University Press, 1970.

Articles in Periodicals

Aceto, Gennaro. "Un amore proibito che diventa un atto naturale e inevitabile." *L'Umanità* 2 April 1980.

Adornato, Ferdinando. "Dieci anni dopo Pasolini: Ha vinto il Palazzo?" *L'Espresso* 27 Oct. 1985.

Anonymous. "L'assassino lo ha finito con l'auto." *Il Tempo* 4 Nov. 1975.

Auglas, Corrado, ed. "Esiste un nuovo corso?" *Sipario* Nov. 1966.

Bocchi, Lorenzo. "Fantasmi pasoliniani in trasferta a Parigi." *Corriere della Sera* 23 Nov. 1984.

Bonino, Guido Davico. "Gassman padre e figlio, scontro avvincente." *La Stampa* 4 Feb. 1986.

———. "'Orgia' l'uomo fra Amore e Morte" *La Stampa* 23 Nov. 1984.

———. "Pasolini, nei 3 sogni del Calderón l'universo-lager della borghesia." *La Stampa* 6 Nov. 1980.

———. "Pasolini, Ronconi e il sogno di 'evadere' dalla borghesia." *La Stampa* 7 June 1978.

———. "Pasolini si specchia in Palach nel suo dramma più sofferto." *La Stampa* 24 Nov. 1985.

C., G. "Pasolini, sulla scena torna al mito d'Edipo." *La Stampa* 1 Feb. 1976.

Cambria, Adele. "Pasolini: un'ipotesi femminista." *Il Giorno* 5 Nov. 1976.

Camon, Ferdinando. "Pasolini: in nome del non-padre." *Il Giorno* 2 Nov. 1976.

Canali, Viola Lou. "Il Teatro di Pasolini." *Sipario* Jan.-Feb. 1985.

Chiaretti, Tommaso. "Tre personaggi senza nome e il piacere delle parole." *La Repubblica* 3 Dec. 1984.

Cibotto, G. A. "Calderón, tre sogni di Pasolini." *Il Gazzettino* 19 June 1987.

De Monticelli, Roberto. "I tre sogni di Pasolini." *Corriere della Sera* 22 June 1978.

_____. "Pasolini 'Orgia' e disperazione." *Corriere della Sera* 3 Dec. 1984.

G., V. R. "Dibutterà il 18 luglio la tragedia di Pasolini." *La Repubblica* 2 June 1981.

Garrone, Nico. "Pasolini come Ian Palach." *La Repubblica* 24–25 Nov. 1985.

Gitlin, Todd. "Hip-deep in Post-modernism." *New York Times* Book Review Section 6 Nov. 1988.

Groppali, Enrico. "Dalla realtà al sogno." *Sipario* Nov. 1979.

_____. "Il teatro di Pasolini come una parabola." *Sipario* Oct. 1979.

Guerrieri, Gerardo. "Pasolini porta Calderón nella Spagna nera." *Il Giorno* 5 July 1977.

Lucchesini, Paolo. "Nel nome del padre di Edipo: Così Gassman ritorna a Pasolini." *La Nazione* 3 Feb. 1986.

_____. "Pasolini e l'ombra di Sofocle." *La Nazione* 25 Jan. 1986.

Marzullo, Gigi. "Quando il potere diventa una tragedia." *Il Mattino* 17 July 1981.

Moravia, Alberto. "Sade per Pasolini un sasso contro la società." *Corriere della Sera* 6 Dec. 1975.

Musati, Cesare. "Calderón, Velazquez, Pasolini." *Sipario* April 1974.

N., M. "Gli scrittori e il teatro." *Sipario* May 1965.

Pasolini, Pier Paolo. "Poeta delle Ceneri." *Nuovi Argomenti* (nuova serie) July-Dec. 1980.

Poesio, Paolo Emilio. "Pilade o la rivoluzione fallita." *La Nazione* 1 Aug. 1981.

Quintavalle, Umberto P. "Pasolini e i giovani di strada." *Il Resto di Carlino* 3 Feb. 1976.

Radice, Raul. "'Orgia' di Pasolini a Torino." *Corriere della Sera* 28 Nov. 1968.

Ronfani, Ugo. "Crudele, scandaloso, tragico Pasolini." *Il Giorno* 3 Dec. 1984.

_____. "Dolce furia di Gassman nel teatro dell'inconscio." *Il Giorno* 3 Feb. 1980.

Rosati, Carlo. "Teatro in forma di martirio." *La Nazione* 17 Nov. 1984.

Schweder, Richard A. "In Paris—Miniskirts of the Mind." *New York Times* Book Review Section 8 Jan. 1989.

Serenellini, Mario, ed. "Ideologia e parola." *Sipario* Dec. 1970.

Siciliano, Enzo. "Gassman nel 'mistero' di Pasolini." *La Stampa* 13 Nov. 1977.

Tian, Renzo. "Conversazione tragica in interno borghese." *Il Messaggero* 13 Nov. 1977.

_____. "Nel cuore violento della coppia borghese." *Il Messaggero* 3 Dec. 1984.

_____. "'Orgia' di Pier Paolo Pasolini fallito esperimento teatrale." *Il Messaggero* 28 Nov. 1968.

Tumbarello, Roberto. "Ammazzando mio figlio, io gli regalo successo." *Oggi* 5 Feb. 1986.

Vignorelli, Giancarlo. "Un viaggio nel mistero tra i borghesi lombardi." *Il Giorno* 20 April 1978.

Zigaina, Giuseppe. "Total Contamination in Pasolini." *Stanford Italian Review*. Fall 1984.

Interviews

Cherif. Personal interview. Rome, 22 Nov. 1985.

Gassman, Vittorio. Interview. *Oggi* 5 Feb. 1986.

Maraini, Dacia. "Il momento della negazione." *Sipario* Aug.-Sept. 1968.

Margherita, Daniela. Personal interview. Rome, 29 Nov. 1985.

Missiroli, Mario. Personal interview. Rome, 14 Dec. 1985.

Pasolini, Pier Paolo. Interview. *Il Messaggero* 2 Nov. 1976.

_____. Interview. *Il Tempo* 28 Mar. 1980.

_____. Interview. *Jonas* Sept. 1985.

_____. "Pier Paolo Pasolini in dialogo con Dacia Maraini." *Vogue* May 1971.

Pelosi, Pino. Interview. *Il Messaggero* 4 Nov. 1975.

Siciliano, Enzo, and Dacia Maraini. Interview. *Sipario* May 1973.
Toccacelli, Mario. Personal interview. Rome, 26 Nov. 1985.
Zigaina, Giuseppe. Personal interview. Cervignano del Friuli, 5 Aug. 1985.

Films

Calderón. Dir. Giorgio Pressburger. RAI, 1981.
Calderón: Laboratorio teatrale di Luca Ronconi. Dir. Miklos Jancso. 1981.
Porcile. Dir. Pier Paolo Pasolini. Film dell'Orso, 1969.

Theatre Programs

" 'Affabulazione' di Pier Paolo Pasolini." Rome: Arte della Stampa, 1985.
" 'Orestiade' di Eschilo: Versione di Pier Paolo Pasolini." Rome: n.p., 1985.
"Pier Paolo Pasolini: 'Orgia.' " Turin: Comlito, 1985.
"Pier Paolo Pasolini 'Una Vita Futura': 'Poesia in forma di azione' e 'Bestia da Stile.' "
    Rome: Graf, 1985.

Personal Letters

Pasolini, Pier Paolo. Personal letter to Don Andrea Carraro, in *Oggi* 13 Nov. 1985.

Index